"This book challenges your assumptions. But stick with it! While making you think, Roberts and Marshall offer hopeful insights for church leaders who are disillusioned, defeated, and discouraged."
—ROGER CROSS, president/CEO, Youth for Christ USA

"If you want to be challenged to think deeply about the practice of ministry today, read this book. Wes and Glenn deliver wise counsel, seasoned by years of pastoral ministry and a keen awareness of the realities that challenge anyone who would minister well in our fast-paced, rapidly changing world."
—STANLEY J. GRENZ, professor of theology, Carey Theological College

"Ready to rethink church? Do you long to experience a church strong with God's presence and aligned with his desires? This book is for you. Expect to face some much-needed corrections about how God wants us to be leaders within his church."
—CRAIG WILLIFORD, PH.D., professor of church leadership and president, Denver Seminary

"God has used *Original Intent* to remind me to give up my life, my dreams, and my ambitions to simply be a servant. Thanks, Wes and Glenn, for reminding us of the early church and the church that will truly have influence. This book is a breath of fresh air."
—MARK SHANER, leadership development, Church of God Ministries

"A full, rich, remarkable, and compelling call to a brand-new, yet 2000-year-old way to be God's family. In the age of the mega-church, here is a mega idea: It's not about size; it's about heart— God's heart."
—C. MCNAIR WILSON, speaker; author, *Raised in Captivity*

"Roberts and Marshall have made a list and they checked it twice: thirteen issues that help Christian leaders cross over the great postmodern divide from Christendom congregations to missional churches."
—REV. PHIL OLSON, vice president, Evangelicals for Social Action; coauthor, *Churches That Make a Difference*

"We live in a society that far too often rewards style and ignores substance. Unfortunately, ministry also falls victim to this superficiality. *Reclaiming God's Original Intent for the Church* calls us back to the depth and richness of our historic faith. A must-read."
—GARY L. GULBRANSON, senior pastor, Westminster Chapel, Bellevue, Washington

"*Original Intent* reads like an open letter to leaders of the church today. Wes and Glenn ask timely questions that penetrate our cultural trappings and awaken vision and thirst for something far better than that for which we have settled."

—Tom Albinson, director of refugee ministries, International Teams, Minneapolis, Minnesota

"Wes Roberts and Glenn Marshall take us back to the radical, difficult, ancient paths of transformed lives. They have put words to a process of obedience that can move the church from a rigid, dutiful, Christian existence to a passionate outpouring of the well that is Christ within us."

—ANGI YORK-CRANE, spiritual director, Solace

"Divine discomfort. If you are a church leader, this is what you will experience when reading this book. Discomfort because whether you are contemporary or traditional, mainline or nondenominational, rediscovering church is not easy. Divine because rediscovering church is good, timely, mysterious, and desperately needed."

—BRIAN PIKALOW, family pastor, Asbury United Methodist Church, Orlando, Florida

"Here is everything you originally believed about ministry and the church but were too force-fed to savor. Welcome home to your first love and your highest calling."

—ROGER THOMPSON, senior pastor, Berean Baptist Church, Burnsville, Minnesota

"For those of us weary of 'playing church,' this remarkable book is like a north star guiding us back to God's original intent for his gathered community. It profoundly stirred my soul and encouraged my heart."

—REV. IAN MORGAN CRON, senior pastor, Trinity Church, Greenwich, Connecticut

RECLAIMING
GOD'S

ORIGINAL
INTENT
for the
CHURCH

WES ROBERTS *and* GLENN MARSHALL

Foreword by Larry Crabb

NAVPRESS®

Bringing Truth to Life

OUR GUARANTEE TO YOU

We believe so strongly in the message of our books that we are making this quality guarantee to you. If for any reason you are disappointed with the content of this book, return the title page to us with your name and address and we will refund to you the list price of the book. To help us serve you better, please briefly describe why you were disappointed. Mail your refund request to: NavPress, P.O. Box 35002, Colorado Springs, CO 80935.

The Navigators is an international Christian organization. Our mission is to reach, disciple, and equip people to know Christ and to make Him known through successive generations. We envision multitudes of diverse people in the United States and every other nation who have a passionate love for Christ, live a lifestyle of sharing Christ's love, and multiply spiritual laborers among those without Christ.

NavPress is the publishing ministry of The Navigators. NavPress publications help believers learn biblical truth and apply what they learn to their lives and ministries. Our mission is to stimulate spiritual formation among our readers.

ISBN 1-57683-407-7

Cover design by Arvid Wallen
Creative team: Nanci McAlister, Brad Lewis, Kathy Mosier, Pat Miller

Some of the anecdotal illustrations in this book are true to life and are included with the permission of the persons involved. All other illustrations are composites of real situations, and any resemblance to people living or dead is coincidental.

Unless otherwise identified, all Scripture quotations in this publication are taken from *THE MESSAGE* ®(MSG). Copyright © 1993, 1994, 1995, 1996, 2000, 2001, 2002. Used by permission of NavPress Publishing Group. Other versions used include: the HOLY BIBLE: NEW INTERNATIONAL VERSION® (NIV®). Copyright © 1973, 1978, 1984 by International Bible Society. Used by permission of Zondervan Publishing House. All rights reserved; quotations designated (NET) are from The Holy Bible: The NET Bible® (New English Translation™). Copyright © 2001 by Biblical Studies Press, L.L.C., www.netbible.com. All rights reserved.

Roberts, Wes.
  Reclaiming God's original intent for the church / Wes Roberts and Glenn Marshall.
    p. cm.
  Includes bibliographical references.
  ISBN 1-57683-407-7
  1. Church. I. Marshall, Glenn, 1953- II. Title.
  BV600.3.R62 2004
  262'.001'7--dc22
                                                    2003020871

Printed in the United States of America

1 2 3 4 5 6 7 8 9 10 / 08 07 06 05 04

FOR A FREE CATALOG OF NAVPRESS BOOKS & BIBLE STUDIES,
CALL 1-800-366-7788 (USA) OR 1-416-499-4615 (CANADA)

Contents

FOREWORD   7

INTRODUCTION: Remembering the Prophets   11

1. It's Not About the Old Ways—
   It's About the Much Older Ways   17

2. It's About Authenticity—Not Size   31

3. It's About Making Disciples—
   Not Simply Recruiting Volunteers   45

4. It's About a Calling—Not a Career   59

5. It's About Character—Not Credentials   71

6. It's About Community—Not Just Management   83

7. It's About Trusting God—Not Technique   99

8. It's About Following the Spirit—Not Mere Strategizing   107

9. It's About Servanthood—Not Power   115

10. It's About Fruit—Not Achievement   127

11. It's About Listening—Not Just Preaching   141

12. It's About Love—Not Being Right   151

13. It's About Our Triune God—Not Us   163

EPILOGUE   177

RESOURCES   181

ACKNOWLEDGMENTS   187

ABOUT THE AUTHORS   191

While they were praying, the place where they were meeting trembled and shook. They were all filled with the Holy Spirit and continued to speak God's Word with fearless confidence.

The whole congregation of believers was united as one — one heart, one mind! They didn't even claim ownership of their own possessions. No one said, "That's mine; you can't have it." They shared everything. The apostles gave powerful witness to the resurrection of the Master Jesus, and grace was on all of them.

And so it turned out that not a person among them was needy. Those who owned fields or houses sold them and brought the price of the sale to the apostles and made an offering of it. The apostles then distributed it according to each person's need.

ACTS 4:31-35

Foreword

In graduate school, I gave up Christianity. At least what I thought was Christianity. It was a good move.

Till then, Christianity for me had been more of an imposed culture, a "here's what we believe and here's how we behave" religion, than a thought-through and personally embraced set of convictions. It had more to do with responsibilities and expectations than with anything vital going on in me or between me and others. Ideas such as freedom and authenticity weren't part of the package. A throbbingly real relationship with Christ wasn't even in sight.

Mostly, I gave it up because it didn't work. The Christianity I knew was a method, a strategy for coaxing a somewhat stingy God to dole out the goodies he could well afford to give, all the while being careful not to get on his bad side. When my elite status as a graduate student gave me the courage to question what I had been taught, I began to think.

I started looking at life more honestly than I ever had before. And I made two discoveries. One, everything I did was moving toward something. I lived not by instinct or reflex reactions but by choice. And that made me wonder what the "something" was I had

chosen to pursue. I had never thought much about that before.

Two, I cared whether people liked me. I couldn't help it. I just did. I couldn't write it off as neurotic insecurity or pretend I really didn't care. I did care, and I cared deeply. I wanted someone to see me exactly as I was and still want to be with me.

So I went into hiding. Because church was the place where the Christianity I had abandoned was still practiced, I lost interest. I still went, out of habit, I guess, but I kept my soul with all its questions in the closet. I hid my true self, which felt empty and alone, behind a more functional self, a decent young man, a hard-working grad student and then competent professional, a devoted husband and father, an occasionally insightful thinker, an all-around reasonably together guy, and a solid Christian.

I had completed my Ph.D. in clinical psychology, I was in an almost thriving practice, and the veneer of Christian appearance was wearing thin. One night at about 1 A.M., I couldn't sleep. I was on our back patio reading Francis Schaeffer.

Suddenly I saw it. I stood up and shouted to no one, "I'm a person. God's a person. We can relate. I want meaning and love. What he is doing matters as nothing else, and he loves me. Life is all about knowing him. Joy is in sight!"

Within minutes, a second outburst came. "I can move toward the meaning I want by living with a community of God-seekers who want to carry out his plan. And I can experience God's love for me by giving it away to others and receiving it from others. And both—finding meaning and experiencing love—can best happen in the church."

At that moment I became a lover of the church. As never before, I saw it as the place where real Christianity—not what I gave up but what I was discovering—could be enjoyed and lived and understood and valued. That happened thirty years ago.

I'm now on the brink of giving up, not Christianity, but

church. Not the true church, not the community of Jesus-followers who journey together toward God for his pleasure and for the sake of others, but the organization that has replaced the living body.

Too often, the whole church event feels like that, like a well-orchestrated event more than a throbbing-with-life community. The raw realism of the Bible is too often sugar-coated with cheerily optimistic promises that God wants you happily married, financially secure, and alive with a sense of adventure and romance. Whether it's a megachurch parading its A-team every Sunday before a packed house of struggling people who are helped to pretend things aren't so bad, or whether it's a single-pastor congregation of a hundred faithful members trying to believe that life can work better than it does, the problem is the same: Too often the church is aiming its people toward self-fulfillment through God's blessings and away from the failure and pain that could bring its people together as the community of the broken but loved and hopeful because of Jesus.

I once gave up Christianity as I knew it and discovered Christianity as the Spirit reveals it. I'm now giving up church as I've experienced it and looking for church as the Spirit designed it.

Reclaiming God's Original Intent for the Church is bringing the picture into focus and creating enough hope to keep me looking. If, like me, you want to trade in illusion for reality, if you're a pastor or church leader or hungry Christian who loves the church and longs to participate in authentic community led by people who are more broken than confident and more Spirit-dependent than naturally talented, if you desire to see the church reformed into a place where character counts more than credentials, where life is lived in humble trust rather than by careful method, where organic growth matters more than organizational growth, where serving nudges aside controlling, then glance at

the chapter titles of this book.

Then read the book. I know Wes Roberts well. I am drawn by his love for the church, by his passion for leaders of all kinds of churches, and by his relentless trust that the Spirit continues to work through the church—big ones, small ones, it doesn't matter. I don't know Glenn Marshall, but Wes tells me he is the kind of leader the church needs. And after several decades of knowing Wes, I trust his judgment.

I began to think when I gave up an imposed understanding of Christianity. Now it's time for all of us to think about the church, in ways as old as the Bible, by giving up what culture has produced. It's time to reclaim God's original intent for the church.

If we do, a lot more people will discover the real meaning of life that survives every crisis, and a lot more people will experience the love that everyone needs. With one heart for Christ and one mind about what it means to live as his body, we just might rediscover church as it was meant to be. This book offers clear guidance for doing just that.

Larry Crabb
Morrison, Colorado

Remembering the Prophets

Count yourselves blessed every time people put you down or throw you out
or speak lies about you to discredit me. What it means is that the truth is
too close for comfort and they are uncomfortable. You can be glad when
that happens—give a cheer, even!—for though they don't like it, I do!
And all heaven applauds. And know that you are in good company.
My prophets and witnesses have always gotten into this kind of trouble.

MATTHEW 5:11-12

It takes all kinds of men and women, all kinds of churches and ministries, all kinds of circumstances to get God's message into our world. The Bible provides many examples of how to live as God's messengers.

As with the Old Testament prophets Haggai and Jeremiah, the size of our current congregations and the breadth and depth of our ministries may differ. But if our triune God calls us to proclaim his Word, we need to pay careful attention to how we differ and the reasons why.

Consider this question: Who was the "successful" prophet— Haggai or Jeremiah? Before you answer, think about your definition of *success*. How would you want your own success defined?

At first glance, Haggai seems more successful. But why? People listened to Haggai. He built coalitions. The temple was rebuilt under his ministry. He got things done.

Now, think about Jeremiah's "success," or lack thereof. During his ministry Judah collapsed and went into exile. When

Jeremiah spoke God's Word, people refused to obey. He was threatened and imprisoned—even left in a cistern to die. All this happened even though he remained faithful to the Lord.

Jeremiah spoke the truth at a time when it wasn't wanted or respected. He opposed and confronted the popular false prophets of his day. He persevered in faithful ministry under demanding circumstances, dealing mainly with obstinate people. So was he a success or a failure?

It's easy to come up with a list of modern-day Haggais. These men and women proclaim God's Word and people respond almost immediately in faith and obedience. They form coalitions, raise money, build buildings for the purposes of God's kingdom. We give praise to God for their ministries.

But we can think of more than a few modern-day Jeremiahs as well. These men and women minister in circumstances that the world, and much of the church, does not consider success-ful. Perhaps you're one of these men and women.

Maybe you minister to a faithful few. Or maybe you have a larger congregation. Perhaps you're the lead pastor—maybe even the only pastor. Or maybe you're in an associate role. Perhaps you're bivocational.

Whatever situation you are in, remember that Jeremiah's calling was just as valid as Haggai's. If you feel more like Jeremiah, con-sider three questions.

First, how do you determine success? Maybe you need to reevaluate what it means to be successful. Success in ministry is commonly measured in terms of attendance, budgets, build-ings, and programs. Do you really believe that's how Jesus measures success?

In what we commonly call the Sermon on the Mount, Jesus held out as examples to follow the prophets who were faithful even though they were insulted and persecuted. We should

expect insults and persecutions. Success is measured in terms of faithfulness, endurance, and perseverance in the calling that God gives to us.

Second, can Jeremiah's ministry be a model of success? We need to recognize that we face the temptation of turning churches into a Haggai-style of ministry. For example, it's easy to talk about moving from smaller congregations to larger ones as a sign of ministry success. We tend to applaud as heroes those who appear to be achieving this kind of success, and we try to emulate what they're doing. Yet for the few pastors who've made this transition, many others have tried but been unable to achieve the "desired results": increased attendance, bigger budgets, multifaceted programs, and grander buildings. However, the attempt to make this transition has left many—both congregations and pastors—bruised, bloodied, and beaten.

Perhaps we need to ask a series of questions that may give us a new perspective:

- Is something wrong with smaller churches remaining small?
- Is something incorrect if budgets don't significantly increase from year to year?
- Is something improper if we're content with the facilities that we currently own?

If we're honest, we'll admit that much of the motivation that drives us to be "bigger and better" is what the Bible calls selfish ambition. We think that if we can just get our churches going and growing, our peers will look up to us with the sense of awe that we have for those who've already "made it." Why can't we instead learn to be content, simply knowing that the Lord has considered us faithful by appointing us to his service (see 1 Timothy 1:12)?

Third, is it possible that smaller is okay? Unfortunately, pastors who labor in smaller churches often hear that their work is insignificant, incorrect, or not in touch with the times. But leading a church has to do with authenticity—no matter the size. Living out the gospel is why the church exists.

As with Jeremiah's ministry, struggle provides the canvas for us to tell God's story honestly and authentically. What our culture needs above all else is a genuine witness to the Lord Jesus Christ that's in tune with the times.

The people of our communities need to be able to look at our churches and see a model of what it means to live under God's reign. Our communities of faith need to demonstrate a clear alternative to the power structures of the world.

Jeremiah serves as an example of this type of demonstration. Against great odds, he stood against the tide of unbelief and remained faithful to his Lord. His story offers us the opportunity to see what authentic ministry is. It gives us the perspective to say to the people of this world that while they find strength in numbers, we find strength in the Lord. While they find power in money, celebrity, or position, we find power in the Holy Spirit.

We need to show the world—which often seeks pleasure apart from God—that we're willing to suffer and sacrifice for a kingdom that cannot be shaken. As a pastor, to serve in the world as Jeremiah did is *not* insignificant. It's a great and holy privilege.

As we've entered the early years of a new millennium, we've all heard the discussions about ministry in a postmodern context. The days of church-as-it-used-to-be are gone. Sadly, many of us haven't recognized the reality of our new context outside of society's norms. Instead of capitalizing on the opportunities this new context grants us, we're looking back at the ground we've lost at the center of our culture.

We're looking in the wrong direction! The vital need of the

present and the future is authentic Christian communities led by broken and transformed leaders devoted to the truth. As men and women called to do the work of the ministry, our challenge is this: Are we willing to be true disciples of Jesus Christ?

While that may seem like a strange question to ask, the truth is that being a disciple has become optional in many of our churches. Perhaps so little discipleship exists in our churches because we've pursued a different course than the one God intended. In order for authentic Christian communities to exist, authentic leaders must exist to lead them—leaders willing to be the Jeremiahs of today.

In order for us to lead the church today and in the future, we need to set aside much of what we've assumed from our past. The vestiges of Christendom are crumbling all around us.[1] We need to learn some important, yet basic, values about ministry.

To learn these values, we need to be willing to think from two perspectives. First, we must unlearn many of the patterns of Christendom ingrained into our souls. Second, we must return to a biblical basis of doing ministry. We must remind ourselves of the basic truths we already know, because these things have grown strangely unfamiliar as we've pursued success in ministry.

God called both Haggai and Jeremiah. Both remained faithful to God's calling, and both served the same Lord. Whether your ministry is more like Haggai's or Jeremiah's is really the choice of God. It's his calling.

As you read on, our hope is that you will find the foundational thoughts suggested in these pages to be helpful and lifegiving—wherever our triune God has called you to serve.

---

[1] The term *Christendom* refers to the institutionalizing of the church that occurred after Constantine's conversion in A.D. 313.

It's Not About the Old Ways—
It's About the Much Older Ways

*You're here to be light, bringing out the God-colors in the world. God is not
a secret to be kept. We're going public with this, as public as a city on a hill.
If I make you light-bearers, you don't think I'm going to hide you under a
bucket, do you? I'm putting you on a light stand. Now that I've put you
there on a hilltop, on a light stand—shine! Keep open house; be generous
with your lives. By opening up to others, you'll prompt people to
open up with God, this generous Father in heaven.*

MATTHEW 5:14-16

Perhaps you've noticed that things aren't the way they used
to be.

Increasingly, the church is becoming marginalized. We're relegated to the fringes of our culture. We struggle to find a voice
in the public square. We're rarely taken seriously. The vast majority of people in our society think the church is irrelevant.

As pastors and church leaders, we feel displaced, lost, frustrated. Our ministries don't match the expectations we had when
we started. We seem to have lost our sense of direction. Things
that used to work don't anymore. Like the ancient Israelites wan-
dering in the desert, we find ourselves in a time of transition.

The good news is that our situation isn't hopeless. The
Sovereign Lord of history is at work in the present as much as he
was in the past. And he's already waiting for us in the future.
Because our hope is in the Lord, we can find encouragement in

much of the confusion we currently find ourselves in.

As we grope our way into the future, we'll learn to come to grips with our marginalization. We'll embrace it and see it as an opportunity for the church to return to her ancient roots in order to reclaim God's original intent for the church. We'll recognize that we're engaged in the mission of God. Mission will no longer be relegated to foreign lands or separated from church life. Instead we'll reengage in mission on the local level. While we won't ignore global concerns, we'll begin to see that mission is done across the street as well as across the world.

Our continued estrangement from the center of our culture will actually help us find our identity in Christ. We'll come to terms with the fact that God sent us into the world for the sake of the world. Learning to be servants will become a priority for us, especially for those of us who are biblical leaders. We'll learn to invest ourselves in the lives of our neighbors and our local communities.

We'll understand that proclaiming the gospel of the kingdom is the responsibility of all Christians, not a few professionals. We'll proclaim this gospel not only in word but also in deed— demonstrating to the people of our local communities what it means to live under the reign of God. We'll acknowledge that not only what we believe but also how we behave—the way we belong to one another in community—makes a difference in how we proclaim the gospel.

We'll realize that we need to identify church membership with discipleship. Growing in Christ will become the expectation of all who belong to our churches. Because this doesn't just happen automatically, we'll learn to train and nurture one another to follow Jesus Christ as Lord in the continuing transformation of our souls.

As Christ becomes our identity, we'll see the need to disengage

from other identities of the world. We'll begin to think instead out of our Christian identity and critique our culture from that perspective. We'll learn to disengage from the power structures of this world in order to serve in the power of weakness. Christ's incarnation will become our way of life. We'll learn to break our conformity to this world and live as the aliens and strangers that we are.

As the new community of Jesus Christ, we'll learn to practice reconciliation as we become one in Christ. We'll celebrate our ethnic, gender, age, and socioeconomic diversity. We'll learn to minister to gays and lesbians with love, hope, and compassion rather than with hatred, fear, and condemnation. We have great hope that the church can actually set the standard for racial reconciliation as well.

We'll engage in the practice of community, our alien status molding us together as a body. We'll find common purpose, ministering in a common place, sharing our personal property for the good of the kingdom. We'll learn to better care for one another in love.

The role of pastors will be remolded according to a more biblical perspective. We'll become postpragmatists, no longer driven by the so-called "proven methods" that promise success in the consumer-driven church business. After we realize that there's more to ministry than finding and employing the proper techniques, we'll repent of our reliance on them and learn to rest again in our dependence on God. We'll learn to become equippers rather than program managers.

Church leaders will learn to suffer and sacrifice for the sake of the flock. We'll continue to lose our positions of status and power within society. We'll no longer be seen as professional managers of religious institutions. Instead, we'll become holy men and women transformed into servant/leaders who will fulfill God's purposes in each generation.

Perhaps you've tried the "church growth" methods. You've likely been to seminars that got you pumped up about trying new techniques and programs, only to find a less than lukewarm reception to these new ideas. Or maybe your church received the ideas warmly, but the results were far less exciting than you'd anticipated.

The problem is that much of our church growth focus is out of touch with the post-Christian, postmodern world. Of course we want our churches to grow. But understanding the times we live in can help us shift our focus to other areas of concern that are more important.

The goal is to help you quit banging your head against a wall. If you've found church growth material to be helpful to you and your church—great! But if you've tried to emulate other growing churches, put new programs into practice without success, and followed models that don't really fit your situation, there's another direction. You don't have to be continually frustrated as you try to make it all work.

That's not your calling.

In order to gain a new perspective, you need to travel into the history of the church to see how the way we've learned to think about church is now out of touch with the reality of our changing world. As you see how the church developed into what it is today, you'll be able to understand why things aren't working the way we expect them to and what we can do about it.

Very simply, the church began as a movement but ended up as an institution. And because the institutional church has lasted for some 1,500 years, we've grown overly familiar with this way of existing. It's ingrained in us. But this institutionalized way of

church—what has been called Christendom—is deteriorating.[1] Because of the way things are now in the context of history, the old institutional mold can't be rebuilt, and it would be unwise to attempt to rebuild it. Biblical Christianity will move on and thrive without it.

In reality, much of the resources, time, and energy now spent by the church are an attempt to rebuild the crumbling ruins of Christendom. For example, we spin our wheels trying to get prayer back in public schools, or we try to keep the Ten Commandments posted in public places. Within the church, we define success in terms of attendance, budgets, programs, and buildings. We don't know what else to do or how else to measure success because we don't know any other way to operate. Christendom is all we know.

But there is another way.

We need to go back to the much older ways—to the time before the church became an institution. This was a time when the church was marginalized, persecuted, and alien—much like it's becoming today. Returning to these much older ways will seem quite new. But if we begin to see that our current situation is similar to those early days, we'll see great opportunities for the present and for the future.

We now have the opportunity, like the early disciples of Jesus, to live in the world like the resident aliens that we are and to demonstrate God's love in tangible ways to the people in our communities. We have the privilege to suffer and sacrifice like the early disciples in order to serve each other and the world. We have the chance to demonstrate love to our enemies, to humble ourselves before others, and to live in such a way that shows we care more for our treasure in heaven than our material possessions on earth. We have the opportunity to live our faith authentically before a watching world.

However, because we're so familiar with the Christendom form of church, we sometimes don't have the capability to see ourselves as resident aliens in this world. It's questionable whether we want to adopt this mindset. We seem far more concerned about building systems of power and structures of permanence on this earth. Much of what we do seems incompatible with the way of Jesus—the way of the Incarnation, the way of weakness and humility, the way of the Cross.

We need a shift in our thinking, and we need to know that it's legitimate to make this shift. If we can recognize that the future we're headed to is similar to the early days of the church—before the church became an institution—then we can form our ministries according to those much older ways. And we don't need to feel threatened, because this much older way is our birthright—our ancient heritage.

Let's look at these two ways of doing church. The first is the "much older way" of the apostolic period. The second way, Christendom, is more familiar to us. The terms *apostolic* and *Christendom* distinguish the ways the church operated, existed, and functioned in different eras.

Maybe you're familiar with those wooden puzzles that form a ball or some other shape. When the ball is disassembled, you can put it together if you have the patience and time to do so. But imagine what that task would be like if some trickster sneaked in and, finding your puzzle dismantled on a table, switched some of the pieces of your puzzle with parts from another puzzle. You could work on that puzzle forever and never put it together.

Think of the two ways of doing church as two puzzles. The old, familiar ways of Christendom are one, and the much older ways of the apostolic period are another. Many of the pieces are not interchangeable.

We begin our journey by going all the way back to the much older ways of the apostolic period—the time before the church gained the favor of the power structures and became institutionalized. Let's look at the pieces that make up this puzzle.

In terms of self-identity, the church at that time had a collective awareness of being the *ecclesia*—those called out from the world. They saw their calling as being set apart from the world— and indeed they were set apart. Others viewed the members of the early church as a bunch of weirdos and strangers. But these weirdos were authentically sold out to Jesus. That's why they were weird. They refused to accept the world's value system. Instead, by grace, they chose to live under God's reign. These early church members refused to participate in the Roman government's pagan rituals; they wouldn't allow Jesus Christ to be assimilated as one of the gods in the pantheon of Roman deities. They could have done so and gained acceptance in their society. But their insistence that Jesus Christ is *the* Lord went against the grain of the culture. The early church was the true countercultural force.

This environment in which the church sprang to life was hostile. Christians were outlawed, persecuted, hunted down, exiled. Some were thrown to lions as a form of entertainment, and others were impaled outside the city of Rome and lit as human streetlamps. It was a crime to be a Christian—an act of treason to declare Jesus Christ as Lord.

Needless to say, becoming a Christian under such circumstances meant making a serious commitment. Discipleship to Jesus Christ was a necessary priority within the church. There was an expectation that to be in the church, a person must undergo conversion. Sometimes this waiting and instruction

period lasted as long as five years before the convert was considered a part of this new community.[2] While we might think this excessive, it shows how discipleship defined what it meant to be a Christian in those early days.

These early disciples had a sense of mission. They saw themselves as sent by God into the world for the sake of the world. Wherever Christians were, that was their place of mission. Local congregations became intent on ministering in both word and deed as witnesses of Jesus Christ. Because the members of this new community were often persecuted and exiled, their witness to Jesus was spread throughout the empire. Mission wasn't the job of a few professional clergy. God gave spiritual gifts so that each member could do his or her part.

The early church's leaders didn't carry on with an air of professionalism. According to the book of Acts, these leaders were common men and women who were called and gifted to shepherd the flock of God. The example of Paul demonstrates that it wasn't uncommon for these leaders to work with their hands to support themselves and their families (see Acts 20:34).

Early Christianity was radical—far more radical than the bland, conservative product we call Christianity today. Early Christians seemed to understand that their faith involved a radical commitment to a wild God who would often lead them to dangerous places.

This new community learned through the hardships of persecution to care for one another's needs. Although they came from different social and ethnic groups, they were bound together by the common purpose of the kingdom of God. They served their local communities with good deeds. They sacrificed and gave of themselves for the service of the kingdom of Christ. They had the conviction that they were a part of God's continuing story of the unfolding of redemption.

Things began to change rather dramatically after the conversion of the emperor Constantine in A.D. 313. Not only did the persecution of Christians cease, but Christianity also gained the official endorsement of the empire.

This began a new chapter in the history of the church and set in place the development of Christendom. This form of church will look familiar to us because it's still around. Let's explore its distinguishing features.

When Christianity became the official religion of the empire, the church became an institution. Everyone living in the Christian empire was regarded as a Christian. Average, everyday citizens of the empire were baptized, catechized, confirmed, and made members of the church. Because people were born into a Christian empire, they claimed the right by birth to receive the blessings of the church. People began to expect the rights and privileges of church membership without the responsibilities of discipleship. As a result, the emphasis on discipleship was lost.

Under Christendom, the church also lost its sense of mission. There was no longer any need to engage in mission locally. Because everyone in the empire was now a "Christian," mission was relegated to the foreign lands—the fringes of the empire—and accomplished by specialists who traveled to far-off places to proclaim the good news. We still feel the fallout of this shift today. Few people in the church think of mission as something done where they live or something that they have any personal involvement or investment in.

During the apostolic period the church was alien and outcast. But Christendom changed that. The environment shifted from hostility to friendly support. Christianity became officially protected and sponsored by the government. This is another lingering

remnant of Christendom in our day. If you aren't sure that's true, answer these questions:

- Would your church survive if it suddenly found its tax-exempt status revoked?
- How would your ministry continue if you had to pay taxes on your church property and revenues?

Soon, the church became the institution of power within society, and the power of the church began to be felt in all areas of life. The Christian story became the metanarrative of the culture.[3] That is, it became the story that gave meaning and explanation to reality. It shaped the dominant worldview.

Christendom also had a profound effect on the leadership of the church. Leaders found themselves with a new status that they hadn't had before, and they soon became the professionals of the church institution. They developed a system of church government in which a cleric could aspire to and attain higher office. Ecclesiastical office became a career path.

For centuries, various forces have been chipping away at the foundation stones of Christendom. Certain teachings of the Reformers of the sixteenth century, such as the authority of the Word of God and the priesthood of all believers, sowed seeds that took root in the church and began to push out some of the institutional blocks from the inside.

But another power, the Enlightenment of the eighteenth century, acted as a battering ram from outside the fortress of Christendom. During the Enlightenment, materialistic science began to replace the Christian story as the world's metanarrative.

For example, prior to the Enlightenment, disasters such as the bubonic plague were seen as an act of God. But afterward, they could be explained scientifically. The plague wasn't caused by God at all—it was a result of germs carried by rats. Scientific law and technique served to explain the universe, and this new approach seemed to make sense. Eventually, even Creation could be explained without a Creator.

This modernism also had effects within the church. The church could be viewed scientifically as well, and professional technicians could employ techniques from the science of church growth. Because modernism defined humans as free and autonomous individuals, consumerism became a power in the world.

Churches eventually saw themselves as local religious franchises competing in the religious marketplace for their market share. Consumers shopped for their church experience. Churches adapted by becoming marketers.

By adopting modernism, the church also adopted a rational approach to theology and apologetics. Truth was now reduced to statements that could be devoid of any practical reality. "Christians" could believe the truth and argue for the truth without ever living out the truth.

The church developed arguments for the existence of God and rational weapons against evolutionary theory. But in the process, it lost a sense of the story of redemption and our place within that story.

Christendom is crumbling and won't be rebuilt. Postmodernism will move us even further away from the possibility of a reconstruction of Christendom as a way of doing church. As Jean-Francois Lyotard, a postmodern philosopher, states, an "incredulity toward metanarratives" now exists.[4] In other words, we've come to a time when people no longer accept *any* overarching story to explain reality. The culture has

no center. Rebuilding Christendom would be like trying to build a house without a foundation.

Instead, we'll have to learn to make a difference from the margins.

The church needs a new paradigm for the way we worship and serve our God. Much of the haze we find ourselves in has to do with being in a time of transition. We're currently "pastoring between the paradigms."[5] The familiar ways of Christendom are ending, and we're groping toward some new way—a way very similar to the much older apostolic way.

We can approach these coming days with hope and confidence in the Sovereign Lord of history. God is at work in all of this! He's at work for our good and for the good of the world.

There's a story about a flock of geese flying south for the winter.[6] As the birds were heading to their winter destination, an early snowstorm forced them to take shelter. They spotted a farm with an open barn, landed, and took shelter in the barn overnight.

The farmer was quite surprised to find that he'd left the barn door open and that the barn was now occupied by a flock of wild geese. But he took compassion on the snowbound birds and provided food for them. The snowstorm lasted several days, and the geese decided to stay put. The farmer continued to feed them.

When the storm finally broke, the geese debated about whether or not to continue on their journey. Because the farmer had been so kind, they decided to stay a while. The farmer thought it was quite a novelty to have a flock of wild geese at his disposal, so he continued to provide for them. The arrangement worked for all parties involved, and the geese decided to stay the winter.

When spring finally arrived, the birds had become acclimated to their new environment. The farm was quite a comfortable place to stay. There were ponds where they could swim, and they had plenty of food. Instead of flying north, the geese decided to stay the spring and summer, too. Before long, this flock of wild geese had become completely domesticated. The seasons came and went, but the geese remained on the farm.

As years went by, the geese began to feel a little guilty about what they'd done to themselves. They'd see other wild geese fly south in the winter and remember the days when they had journeyed forth with the same reckless abandon. So to assuage their guilt they devised a plan. Every year as winter approached, the eldest goose stood before the throng of geese to tell the story of the former days when they used to fly south for the winter. He recounted the trials and difficulties as well as the great joys they encountered when they were wild.

As we, the church, head into the future, we can't settle for domestication. We can't settle for just hearing about the glory days of the church. Instead, we must return to the much older ways. We were born to be wild.

---

[1] See Loren B. Mead, *The Once and Future Church: Reinventing the Congregation for a New Mission Frontier* (Bethesda, Md.: The Alban Institute, 1991), and Mike Regele and Mark Schulz, *Death of the Church* (Grand Rapids, Mich.: Zondervan, 1995).

[2] Alan Kreider, *The Change of Conversion and the Origin of Christendom* (Harrisburg, Pa.: Trinity Press International, 1999), p. 24.

[3] For an excellent discussion on understanding the term metanarrative, please refer to Leonard Sweet, Brian McLaren, and Jerry Haselmayer, *A Is for Abductive: The Language of the Emerging Church* (Grand Rapids, Mich.: Zondervan, 2003), p. 193.

[4] Jean-Francois Lyotard, *The Postmodern Condition: A Report on Knowledge* (Minneapolis: University of Minnesota Press, 1984), p. xxiv.

[5] Greg Ogden, "Pastoring Between the Paradigms," *The Pastor's Update*, vol. 18 (Pasadena, Calif.: Fuller Theological Seminary, 1998), audiocassette.

[6] This story has been attributed to Søren Kierkegaard, and it certainly sounds like something he would have written. But in searching his writings, we've been unable to find the source.

It's About Authenticity—
Not Size

Brothers, think of what you were when you were called. Not many of you
were wise by human standards; not many were influential; not many were
of noble birth. But God chose the foolish things of the world to shame the
wise; God chose the weak things of the world to shame the strong. He chose
the lowly things of this world and the despised things—and the things that
are not—to nullify the things that are, so that no one may boast before him.
It is because of him that you are in Christ Jesus, who has become for us
wisdom from God—that is, our righteousness, holiness and redemption.
Therefore, as it is written: "Let him who boasts boast in the Lord."

1 CORINTHIANS 1:26-31, NIV

*F*ace it: You're under a lot of pressure. Maybe your denomination or church association tends to push you one way or another. Your peers probably expect you to carry out their suggestions. And the people in the pews might have differing opinions about how you should do ministry and what results your ministry should produce. But perhaps the biggest pressure you face comes from your personal expectations about ministry.

Stop for a few moments and ponder your own expectations for ministry. What are you attempting to accomplish in your work? What do you dream about?

If you look at the seminars, books, and resources that occupy our time, you'd think that attendance, budgets, programs, and buildings are top priorities in the church business. You attend seminars meant to help you break through one barrier or

another. You implement programs designed to help the church raise more money. You read books that teach how to grow a church. All of these assume that bigger is better.

Early in my ministry when I (Wes) was getting my feet wet as a youth pastor, I dreaded going to the monthly denominational ministers' breakfasts. Nothing was more boring. When the senior pastor I was working with let me know that he was bored, too, I learned an important lesson about being part of a group. He reasoned that it was good to attend even if the only reason was to encourage others.

At every single breakfast meeting, one of the pastors would come up to my senior pastor and pompously ask, "Well, Bob, how big's your church now?" With amusement, I waited for the answer because it was always the same: "You know, Henry, it's still 37,000 square feet." Without skipping a beat—and not listening to the comment—Henry would seek out another pastor and ask the same question.

I would then hear Bob ask the other pastors about their spouse or kids, inquire how they were doing with a difficult issue in their church, engage them in some joint mission project, or ask if the men from their church could help with a needed paint job. Think about the questions people ask about your church. What questions do you ask when you're with other church leaders?

Of course, we want to see our churches grow for many reasons. One reason is that money is a practical commodity for doing the work of the kingdom, and more people usually means more financial and human resources to accomplish what we'd like to do as we reach out to the community.

And if bigger means more people following Jesus, of course bigger is better. We all ought to share the heart of God "who wants all men to be saved and to come to a knowledge of the truth" (1 Timothy 2:4, NIV). We're not arguing against church

growth. Church growth may, in fact, be a fine result of your work. But it shouldn't be the goal of your work. It's not heresy to say that you have more important things to consider as a pastor.

There's something far more important than the size of your church. You know this. But it bears repeating that it should be the goal of your church—regardless of size—to be an authentic witness for Jesus Christ and the gospel of his kingdom. Sadly, that goal often gets lost in the frantic push to grow.

We need to get back to basics regularly—back to the original intent for the church. What does it mean to be an authentic witness for Jesus Christ? First, being a witness is a matter of *being*.

Being an authentic witness has to do with your character—the way you exist before a watching world. Are you sincerely merciful? Do you love justice? Are you generous? Are you sacrificial with regard to the work of the kingdom? Do you treat those who disagree with you with love and respect? Are you forgiving? These questions have to do with your authentic witness to the world in terms of your identity as an individual and a church leader and the identity of your church as the people of God. This is a matter of holiness—personal and corporate.

Holiness—doesn't it seem that this word has fallen out of favor? Holiness may *seem* a little out of place. But it's exactly what we need to recapture if we're going to be authentic witnesses for Jesus Christ and his kingdom.

Personal holiness is crucial. E. M. Bounds makes the point this way:

> The work of God in the world is the implantation, the growth, and the perfection of holiness in His people.

Keep this always in mind. But we might ask just now, is this work advancing in the church? Are men and women being made holy? Is the present-day church engaged in the business of making men and women holy? This is not a vain and speculative question. It is practical, pertinent, and all-important. . . . There is no shutting our eyes to the real facts. If the church does not do this sort of work, if the church will not advance its members in holiness of heart and life, then all our show of activities and all our display of church work are a delusion and a snare.[1]

The apostle Peter wrote, "Just as he who called you is holy, so be holy in all you do; for it is written: 'Be holy, because I am holy'" (1 Peter 1:15-16, NIV). Personal holiness has to do with otherness. God is other than the rest of creation. And he calls his people to be something other than the world.

This isn't a call to some new form of monasticism. We're to remain in the world—but we're not of the world. Jesus said this as he prayed to his Father:

> "I gave them your word;
> The godless world hated them because of it,
> Because they didn't join the world's ways,
> Just as I didn't join the world's ways.
> I'm not asking that you take them out of the world
> But that you guard them from the Evil One.
> They are no more defined by the world
> Than I am defined by the world.
> Make them holy—consecrated—with the truth;
> Your word is consecrating truth.
> In the same way that you gave me a mission in the world,
> I give them a mission in the world.

I'm consecrating myself for their sakes
So they'll be truth-consecrated in their mission."
(John 17:14-19)

The church is the people of God, called out from the world.
Being called out has the connotation of being different—being
other from the rest of the world. If this is true, how do we deal
with this sobering statement from George Barna: "Believers are
largely indistinguishable from non-believers in how they think
and live"?[2]

Instead of being conformed to Christ, it's too easy to become
conformed to the culture we live in. We've succumbed to worldliness. A recent declaration makes this point:

> As evangelical faith becomes secularized, its interests
> have been blurred with those of the culture. The result
> is a loss of absolute values, permissive individualism,
> and a substitution of wholeness for holiness, recovery
> for repentance, intuition for truth, feeling for belief,
> chance for providence, and immediate gratification for
> enduring hope. Christ and his cross have moved from
> the center of our vision.[3]

Personal holiness should lead to corporate holiness. The apostle
Peter spoke to this issue when he said, "But you are a chosen
people, a royal priesthood, a holy nation, a people belonging to
God, that you may declare the praises of him who called you
out of darkness into his wonderful light" (1 Peter 2:9, NIV). Our
nature as the church is inseparably connected to our mission as
the church. Our witness to the world flows from who we are as

God's chosen people—people belonging to God.

Craig Van Gelder illustrates this point with his description of the demonstration plots used by extension agents in rural Iowa:

> Growing up on a farm in rural Iowa provided me with an object lesson for understanding the church's being mission by nature. Each county in the state employed an extension agent to work with farmers. . . . As new farming technologies, seeds, and fertilizers became available, the extension agents introduced these to the farmers. My dad, like many farmers, was often hesitant to accept the innovations. One of the methods extension agents used to gain acceptance of these innovations was demonstration plots.
>
> A strip of land, usually along a major roadway, was selected as a demonstration plot, where a new farming method, seed, or fertilizer was used to raise a crop.
>
> It was not uncommon for farmers to remain skeptical throughout the summer as the crops grew. But there was always keen interest in the fall when the crop was harvested. Invariably, the innovation performed better than the crops in the surrounding fields. By the next year, many of the farmers, including my dad, would be using the innovation as if it had been their idea all along.
>
> The church is God's demonstration plot in the world. Its very existence demonstrates that his redemptive reign has already begun. Its very presence invites the world to watch, listen, examine, and consider accepting God's reign as a superior way of living.[4]

Authentic Christian witness means that you and your church become a demonstration plot of God's kingdom for the world to

see. It's a matter of being different in terms of character, integrity, and values. It's a matter of holiness.

The authenticity of this kind of witness is closely associated with the gospel that you proclaim. If you were merely peddling some form of religious philosophy, then character, integrity, and values wouldn't matter much. Your message would just need to be more interesting or self-pleasing than other messages you were competing with.

But you proclaim the gospel of the kingdom! It's about living within the sphere of God's reign. This message sets you apart as one of God's distinct people. It's a gospel that requires repentance and that promises a new creation. As Lesslie Newbigin stated so well, "The church is not an end in itself. 'Church growth' is not an end in itself. The church is only true to its calling when it is a sign, an instrument, and a foretaste of the kingdom."[5]

Does the character of your life live up to the messages you preach? Are you a living demonstration of the gospel of the kingdom? What are you and your church willing to sacrifice for the sake of the gospel? Are you willing to give up the bigger and better to cultivate holiness in yourself and your people? These are important questions for anyone working within the church.

Second, we need to remember that authentic Christian witness isn't just about being—it's also about doing. Jesus made this clear when he spoke to his disciples about the moment when he'll return:

> "When he finally arrives, blazing in beauty and all his
> angels with him, the Son of Man will take his place on
> his glorious throne. Then all the nations will be

arranged before him and he will sort the people out, much as a shepherd sorts out sheep and goats, putting sheep to his right and goats to his left.

"Then the King will say to those on his right, 'Enter, you who are blessed by my Father! Take what's coming to you in this kingdom. It's been ready for you since the world's foundation. And here's why:

> I was hungry and you fed me,
> I was thirsty and you gave me a drink,
> I was homeless and you gave me a room,
> I was shivering and you gave me clothes,
> I was sick and you stopped to visit,
> I was in prison and you came to me.'

"Then those 'sheep' are going to say, 'Master, what are you talking about? When did we ever see you hungry and feed you, thirsty and give you a drink? And when did we ever see you sick or in prison and come to you?' Then the King will say, 'I'm telling the solemn truth: Whenever you did one of these things to someone overlooked or ignored, that was me—you did it to me.'" (Matthew 25:31-40)

Authentic Christian witness involves both inward and outward behavior. The inward focus has to do with the way you practice discipleship with others within the community of faith—setting aside time to listen, pray, help and encourage, care, study the Scripture, and worship and fellowship with one another. But there's also an outward focus—reaching beyond the community of faith with deeds of love, mercy, and justice. You proclaim the good news of the kingdom not only with actions but also with

words, as Newbigin clearly describes:

> What is required of us is faithfulness in word and deed,
> at whatever the cost; faithfulness in action for truth, for
> justice, for mercy, for compassion; faithfulness in speak-
> ing the name of Jesus when the time is right, bearing
> witness, by explicit word as occasion arises, to God
> whom we are and whom we serve. There are situations
> where the word is easy and the deed is costly; there are
> situations where the deed is easy and the word is
> costly. Whether in word or in deed, what is required in
> every situation is that we be faithful to him who said to
> his disciples: "As the Father sent me, so I send you,"
> and showed them his hands and his side.[6]

When it comes to authentic Christian witness, the size of your
congregation is irrelevant. What is relevant is to be who you say
you are and to live out of that reality. You need to give yourself
permission to stop chasing after numbers and more intentionally
chase after God.

Speaking of chasing, a while ago I (Wes) was outside finish-
ing my daily ten thousand steps of exercise, which I am committed to doing to maintain my health. The day had been
particularly busy and stressful at times as I attended to phone
calls from a variety of ministry leaders who were in the midst of
personal and/or organizational chaos.

It was a great Colorado evening—warm, with a gentle
breeze. Couples and families were enjoying the chance to be out
on the hiking and biking trails of our community. But as I
rounded the turn for home I heard some kids screaming.

Two little girls and a boy—siblings, I assumed—had been
playing with an orange ball in their backyard when it bounced

over their fence and headed onto one of the busiest streets in our area. The kids, peering over their fence, watched their ball roll into traffic.

For a moment I almost walked by. After all, it was only a ball, which could be replaced. But I'd just been working through thoughts about being authentic and living the gospel—not just knowing it. In a quick moment, the Spirit whispered in my soul, "Don't walk past. You have a congregation of three watching you."

Before I realized it, I was in the middle of the road with traffic bearing down, chasing an orange ball. After dodging speeding cars and hearing a few choice words yelled my way, I got the ball. I threw it back over the fence to the three children. "Here you go. Have fun," I said as I went tromping on toward home. Within a few steps I heard the boy calling, "Mister, mister!" He waved me back to his spot at the fence, where I could see his mom standing in the doorway to their deck. His sisters looked over the fence, too.

He said, "Thank you. That was an important ball for my littlest sister. We gave it to her for her birthday this weekend." I could see it was important to him, too. I looked at the youngest child, and as she finished wiping the last remnants of tears from her face, she very quietly said, "Thank you, mister."

Authenticity can happen in many mystical, good, solid ways. What are the small but important things you, too, need to be paying attention to within your own congregation? Listen for the Spirit to tell you when to go after the orange balls that come your way.

Do you hope to see people added to your community of faith? Of course. The problem is that when we focus on numbers, our hearts are turned away from the radical requirements of the kingdom of God. Focusing on numbers doesn't lead us to a discipleship that results in a growing personal holiness.

Encouraging others to focus on authentic Christian witness is

radical. It calls for a total dependency on God. It calls for an uncompromising belief in the necessity of becoming disciples in such a way that those we encounter become holy, alive, authentic people. It requires a changed life. It may even signal a call for a revolution in the way church life is carried out.[7] Søren Kierkegaard stated:

> The established Church is far more dangerous to Christianity than any heresy or schism. We play at Christianity. We all use the orthodox Christian termi-nology—but everything, everything without character. Yes, we are simply not fit to shape a heresy or a schism. There is something frightful in the fact that the most dangerous thing of all, playing at Christianity, is never included in the list of heresies and schisms.[8]

The point is this: Unless we focus on authenticity, we fall into the danger of merely "playing at Christianity." Christianity must be authentic or it isn't Christianity.

Henri Nouwen echoes these thoughts with words that need to be read at least once a year to help us keep our focus:

> Real theological thinking, which is thinking with the mind of Christ, is hard to find in the practice of the min-istry. Without solid theological reflection, future leaders will be little more than pseudo-psychologists, pseudo-sociologists, pseudo-social workers. They will think of themselves as enablers, facilitators, role models, father or mother figures, big brothers or big sisters, and so on, and thus join the countless men and women who make a living by trying to help their fellow human beings to cope with the stresses and strains of everyday living.

But that has little to do with Christian leadership because the Christian leader thinks, speaks, and acts in the name of Jesus, who came to free humanity from the power of death and open the way to eternal life. To be such a leader it is essential to be able to discern from moment to moment how God acts in human history and how personal, communal, national, and international events that occur during our lives can make us more and more sensitive to the ways in which we are led to the cross and through the cross to the resurrection.[9]

If your focus is on the bigger and better, it's quite possible that your view of authentic ministry will be skewed in ways you may not even realize. The drive to be bigger and better has pressured us, as pastors, to demand the wrong things of our people and ourselves.

We concentrate on programs that foster church growth and activities that draw crowds instead of values that will produce holiness in ourselves and in our people. We hold ourselves up to standards like excellence and professionalism and rely on sociology, business methods, and marketing to achieve them. We may be able to produce slick advertisements and well-orchestrated worship services, but where's the life change? Where's the transformation? Where's the community? Where's the devotion to Christ? Where are the disciples of Jesus?

We need to come to the place where we realize that authenticity begins with us. We can't give what we don't have. We need to trust in God rather than the newest techniques or latest fads. It's time for us to seek a change of heart so that each of us can truly believe deep inside that it's not about size—it's about authenticity.

Be looking for the orange balls that cross your path.

1 E. M. Bounds, *Essentials of Prayer* (New Kensington, Pa.: Whitaker House, 1994), pp. 71-73.

2 George Barna, *Growing True Disciples* (Colorado Springs, Colo.: WaterBrook Press, 2001), p. 14.

3 *The Cambridge Declaration of the Alliance of Confessing Evangelicals* (Philadelphia: Alliance of Confessing Evangelicals, 1996), p. 3. This is available from the Alliance of Confessing Evangelicals. Their website is www.christianity.com/ace. We offer this quotation as an illustration of how the church has succumbed to worldliness, although we do not necessarily agree with all the details that it expresses.

4 Craig Van Gelder, *The Essence of the Church: A Community Created by the Spirit* (Grand Rapids, Mich.: Baker, 2001), pp. 99-100.

5 Lesslic Newbigin, *Mission in Christ's Way: A Gift, a Command, an Assurance* (New York: Friendship Press, 1988), p. 12.

6 Newbigin, p. 14.

7 We encourage you to read Dwight Edwards, *Revolution Within: A Fresh Look at Supernatural Living* (Colorado Springs, Colo.: WaterBrook Press, 2001).

8 Charles E. Moore, ed., *Provocations: Spiritual Writings of Kierkegaard* (Farmington, Pa.: The Plough Publishing House of the Bruderhof Foundation, 1999), p. 227.

9 Henri J. M. Nouwen, *In the Name of Jesus: Reflections on Christian Leadership* (New York: Crossroad, 1998), pp. 65-67.

It's About Making Disciples— Not Simply Recruiting Volunteers

My counsel for you is simple and straightforward: Just go ahead with what
you've been given. You received Christ Jesus, the Master; now live him.
You're deeply rooted in him. You're well constructed upon him.
You know your way around the faith. Now do what you've been taught.
School's out; quit studying the subject and start living it!
And let your living spill over into thanksgiving.

COLOSSIANS 2:6-7

*D*allas Willard has written some rather startling comments about discipleship. In *The Spirit of the Disciplines*, he states:

For at least several decades the churches of the Western world have not made discipleship a condition of being a Christian. One is not required to be, or to intend to be, a disciple in order to become a Christian, and one may remain a Christian without any signs of progress toward or in discipleship. Contemporary American churches in particular do not require following Christ in his example, spirit, and teachings as a condition of membership— either of entering into or continuing fellowship of a denomination or local church. Any exception to this

claim only serves to highlight its general validity and make the general rule more glaring. So far as the visible Christian institutions of our day are concerned, discipleship clearly is optional.[1]

More startling is the truth of his comments. It makes us wonder, *How did we get here from where we used to be?*

Jesus made some radical statements about what it means to follow him. He said that we must deny ourselves and daily pick up our cross and follow him (see Luke 9:23). Following him involves a total, whole-life commitment to his lordship: "Any of you who does not give up everything he has cannot be my disciple" (Luke 14:33, NIV). Jesus is clear about the cost of following him. How did these requirements of discipleship somehow evaporate from the consciousness of the church?

The early church seemed to understand the cost of discipleship. Within the New Testament, we see evidence of persecution and suffering for the sake of following Jesus. We see the apostle Paul as an extreme example of what it means to follow him. But the Bible speaks of others as well who were imprisoned or exiled for the cause of Christ. And history is replete with examples of people who surrendered all for their faith in Jesus.

Waves of persecution were common for the church during its first three hundred years. It's interesting to read the letter of Pliny, written around A.D. 112, to the Emperor Trajan regarding Pliny's trials and executions of Christians in Bithynia. Note the matter-of-fact way he writes of torturing two deaconesses in the church in order to force their confessions. He states, "I thought it more necessary, therefore, to find out what truth there was in this by applying torture to two maidservants, who were called deaconesses. But I found nothing but a depraved and extravagant superstition."[2]

While this was a common experience for the church in its early days, the church didn't merely survive—it thrived, evidenced by the following statistics: "If, as many scholars now agree, at the time of the emperor Constantine's legalization of Christianity in 312, approximately 10 percent of the imperial population belonged to the Christian church, then during the previous three centuries the churches statistically grew at an average of 40 percent per decade."[3]

Think about that statement. During a time when Christianity was outlawed and Christians were the outcasts of society, Christianity grew. And it grew without big-screen presentations and air-conditioned church buildings with comfy seats. Without seeker services. Without evangelistic crusades and programmed gospel presentations.

Instead, Christians met in secret to worship together. In fact, deacons guarded the door to screen people attempting to come in.[4] As one scholar explained, "Christian worship was designed to enable Christians to worship God. It was not designed to attract non-Christians; it was not 'seeker sensitive,' for seekers were not allowed in."[5]

How did Christianity thrive? The character of those early Christians was so engaging that they couldn't be ignored. They possessed a character born out of being disciples of Jesus Christ. They understood that through many hardships they would enter the kingdom of God. Living as aliens and strangers, what a difference they made in their world!

In our day, we've learned to rely on modern conveniences and a myriad of programs and tools. But as Dallas Willard says, we lack the character of being disciples of Jesus.

Things began to change for the church after the conversion of Constantine and the official recognition of Christianity as the religion of the empire. We've been calling that change "Christendom."

Under Christendom, discipleship was no longer a requirement for belonging to the church. People became a part of the church simply by being born into a Christian nation. Membership in the church was attained merely by undergoing the rituals of baptism and confirmation and by participating in the church's other sacraments. People accomplished this without much change in character and without any real commitment to Jesus— without any real conversion.

The world has changed many times in the past 1,500 years, and people's attitudes have changed with it. In its last stage, Christendom began to be shaped by the modern ideas of the Enlightenment. This movement defined people as free and independent individuals. The church adopted this idea about human nature and began to see the church in terms of a voluntary society.

Much of the seeker-driven mentality that directs so many of the current practices in modern Christianity is based on these assumptions about human nature and the need to recruit or induce volunteers to show up and join in. If we can find a way to make Christianity appealing and if we meet their felt needs, free and independent individuals might just find church to be an organization they would choose to belong to.

This whole concept of volunteerism not only affects the way we recruit new members; it also affects the way we raise up leaders in the church. For too many churches, there's no sense of developing leaders according to the combination of their spiritual gifting and their natural strengths for leadership. Most congregations don't take seriously the equipping of men and women based on that combination.

Churches function through their people. As we know from

Ephesians, the pastor/teacher is called to equip the saints to do the work of the ministry. Churches need leaders who are nurtured and trained. But too many churches don't have an intentional process of developing leaders from the soul out. Instead, they approach the process of leadership by searching for people who are available and willing to serve in various positions and boards of the church. For many churches—especially smaller churches—any warm body will do. Leadership development dissolves into filling open positions with volunteers who aren't trained and encouraged according to their gifts and strengths. In many cases, discipleship isn't even a requirement for these positions.

Churches of all sizes pay a price for tolerating such uninformed leadership. Consistent, intentional, character-building, life-transforming, team-building leadership development isn't addressed. Church leaders often do their duties without clear expectations and affirmation, either biblical or from within the body.

Do you see how far we have drifted from the Lord's calling for disciples? There is a great difference between a volunteer and a disciple. A volunteer gets to set her own schedule. A volunteer calls his own shots. A volunteer comes and goes as she pleases. A volunteer gets to be his own boss.

But a disciple has a Lord. Jesus never told us to go and recruit volunteers—he told us to go and make disciples. He doesn't call us to pitch in—he calls us to surrender all as we work together in his church.

In many cases, we are guilty of the charge of performing a "bait and switch." We draw people into our churches by appealing to individualism. We tell them that it's all about them and their likes and needs. And then when they're ready to make a

formal commitment, we reverse course and say that it's not about them at all. Instead, it's all about Jesus and following him. It seems that individualism and the command of Christ to deny ourselves are mutually exclusive.

The gospel of Matthew tells a story about what it means to follow Jesus. Matthew records the content of Jesus' preaching as "Repent, for the kingdom of heaven is near" (Matthew 4:17, NIV). Interestingly, immediately following this is the call of his disciples. Jesus' call and the disciples' responses reveal something of what it means to live under the reign of God as followers of Christ.

We see, for example, that discipleship involves a leaving. That is, it involves repentance. Like Peter and Andrew, James and John, who left their nets to follow Jesus, we must also leave something to follow him. To borrow the content of Jesus' message, we must "repent and believe the good news" (Mark 1:15).

The sad reality of substituting volunteerism for discipleship is that a person can participate without ever leaving anything. Many people live under the delusion that they can have the blessings of Christ without living a transformed life.

But discipleship requires more than merely leaving. We must leave to follow Jesus. This involves at least three important points. First, discipleship means living in a relationship with the living Lord Jesus Christ. We can't follow him if he's nowhere in sight. We receive the vitality we need for our lives through union with Christ—living in relationship with him.

Second, following Jesus has to do with obeying all that he has commanded. In the Great Commission, Jesus told us that if we love him, we will keep his commandments. We can't be disciples of Jesus unless we're willing to live in faithful obedience to him.

There seems to be a lack of understanding on this point in our day. We've allowed people to believe that Christ exists for their needs, instead of pointing out their need to come to him as

Lord. We've allowed people to believe that they've made a commitment to Christ through their acceptance of him or through some act of religiosity, without them actually making a commitment to the living Lord and comprehending what that commitment entails. The Bible is clear that life without repentance—a life without obedience to Christ—will keep us from inheriting the kingdom of God:

> Don't you realize that this is not the way to live? Unjust people who don't care about God will not be joining in his kingdom. Those who use and abuse each other, use and abuse sex, use and abuse the earth and everything in it, don't qualify as citizens in God's kingdom. A number of you know from experience what I'm talking about, for not so long ago you were on that list. Since then, you've been cleaned up and given a fresh start by Jesus, our Master, our Messiah, and by our God present in us, the Spirit. (1 Corinthians 6:9-11)

Third, following Jesus involves an imitation of his life. Jesus is your example. Discipleship means engaging in a process through which you mature and become more and more like him. God is at work, molding you into the image of his Son. Following Jesus involves the practice of spiritual disciplines in your life.

Because life can be so cluttered that it takes you away from the basics, allow us to remind you that *discipleship* comes from *discipline*. In its best sense, this word refers to training, instruction, and learning. The Scriptures refer many times to discipline and the gaining of wisdom and understanding.

Discipleship is a journey—it's a way of life. Peter and Andrew, James and John didn't go on a picnic or an extended vacation. They were in it for the long haul. Discipleship is a

whole-life commitment to the whole person of Jesus.

This is one reason the apostle Paul likens marriage to the relationship that exists between Christ and his church. When a man and woman get married, they don't get to choose the parts they wish to eradicate in the other. They marry each other, warts and all. They make a whole-life commitment to a whole person.

Discipleship to Christ is similar. Sometimes the demands of discipleship are difficult. Sometimes our flesh cries out for us to go in more self-serving, self-absorbed directions. But in this life, Jesus remains Lord. You must continue to follow him. You have to ask yourself, "How can I not follow the Lord when he gave what he did for me?" Because of his commitment and by his grace, you can devote yourself to him.

Being on this journey with Jesus means that you'll always feel unsettled in this life. That's why it requires faith to live it. You can't settle down here because you're headed for a home that is not of this world. You'll always be an alien and stranger in this world, on your way to a heavenly destination that God promises you—one that will someday be revealed to you.

My new friend, Ian Morgan Cron, is both an exceptional young pastor and a tremendous musician. When I (Wes) first heard his self-produced CD, *Sacred Hunger,* both my wife and I were smitten with the second cut on the disc, "I Want to Go Home." Words without the awesome music don't do justice to the song. But allow the poetry and rich meaning of the words to sink in for a bit.

"I Want to Go Home"
This Irish coast is breaking my heart tonight
A mystical yearning, an ache in my soul

Each crashing wave reminds me
I'm living in exile

I want to go home
I want to be with my Father
Run right by his side through all his fields of grace
Yes, I love my life
But isn't it right
To want to go home

Is it so wrong to want the invisible?
A time and a place where you finally belong
I could go on in this world
With just one taste of eternity

I want to go home
I want to be with my Father
Run right by his side through all his fields of grace
Yes, I love my life
But isn't it right
To want to go home

This "now but not yet" leaves me divided
Walking on earth when my soul wants to fly
But I know this journey I'm on is built on this sacred
    hunger

And . . .
I want to go home
I want to be with my Father
Run right by his side through all his fields of grace
Yes, I love my life

But isn't it right
To want to go home[6]

When we recover the necessity of discipleship, we rediscover what it means to be a Christian. Discipleship provides us with a working definition of what being a Christian is about. Again, Dallas Willard provides great insight:

> The word "disciple" occurs 269 times in the New Testament. "Christian" is found three times and was first introduced to refer precisely to the disciples—in a situation where it was no longer possible to regard them as a sect of the Jews (Acts 11:26). The New Testament is a book about disciples, by disciples, and for disciples of Jesus Christ.[7]

Discipleship was the essential requirement of the apostolic church. We must return to this requirement as we probe forward into the future. It defines Christianity and what we must expect of one another within the community of faith.

Of course, this is all related to our mission as the church of Jesus Christ. It's about who and what we are before the eyes of the watching world. Authentic Christianity can only exist in a community of faith where biblical discipleship is the norm and where the rank and file is wholly committed to Jesus Christ. Only such a community can serve as the hermeneutic of the gospel.[8]

Sadly, the church of our day has lost sight of this. We've focused on worship attendance and drawing large crowds—often to the detriment of disciple making. Some churches have become effective at increasing attendance simply by discounting

the cost of discipleship, by offering cheap grace, or by making the demands of the gospel more palatable to the sensibilities of sinful human beings.

The pressure for success—the "bigger and better" kind—has made many of us buckle under the tyranny of the numbers. It's deceived us into thinking that we are faithful to the Great Commission if we simply draw a crowd. But the Great Commission requires that we make disciples—not just add up numbers of recruited volunteers.

Do you remember the Great Commission? Allow us to refresh your memory.

> Meanwhile, the eleven disciples were on their way to Galilee, headed for the mountain Jesus had set for their reunion. The moment they saw him they worshiped him. Some, though, held back, not sure about *worship,* about risking themselves totally.
>
> Jesus, undeterred, went right ahead and gave his charge: "God authorized and commanded me to commission you: Go out and train everyone you meet, far and near, in this way of life, marking them by baptism in the threefold name: Father, Son, and Holy Spirit. Then instruct them in the practice of all I have commanded you. I'll be with you as you do this, day after day after day, right up to the end of the age." (Matthew 28:16-20)

Please hear this loud and clear: *We are not against numbers.* Just look at how many people were added to the church in the New Testament account of Acts. All people count. Nothing is wrong with a megachurch being megasized. We need churches of *all* sizes.

But having looked at a number of studies on church size, let us remind you that the *average* church size in North America is somewhere between 110 and 135 people. There are more than 300,000 churches in the United States and Canada. Sincerely thank God for them all—no matter what their size.

There is no justification for not being faithful and fruitful in proclaiming the gospel. Yet, in our consumer-driven, twenty-first-century Christianity, we've too often focused on numbers and haven't paid attention to Jesus' requirement to make disciples. According to the Lord, we can't consider ourselves successful simply because we draw a crowd. Much more is required of us.

We're thankful for megachurches that have placed an emphasis on discipleship. These are the Haggai ministries we spoke of in the introduction. We need to take care not to feel envious of such churches. Let's not judge them as if they have done something wrong to achieve such success. Instead, let's thank God for what he has given them and for their ministry in his name.

At the same time, let's learn to appreciate the many Jeremiahs among us. Let's commend them for toughing it out and making disciples in their difficult ministries. Let's not judge them as if they're failures. Far more may be going on in their ministries than we realize. Let's not tempt them to use any measurement of success other than what God has given us.

The early church understood the cost and the reality of discipleship. These were people who left their former ways of life to follow Jesus and live under his lordship. They became aliens and strangers in the world. Many were persecuted or became martyrs because of their faith. As we pastor between the paradigms, let's learn to follow their examples.

1 Dallas Willard, *The Spirit of the Disciplines: Understanding How God Changes Lives* (New York: HarperSanFrancisco, 1990), pp. 258-259.

2 The entire text of this letter and Trajan's response is found in Henry Bettenson, ed., *Documents of the Christian Church* (London: Oxford University Press, 1956), pp. 3-6.

3 Alan Kreider, *The Change of Conversion and the Origin of Christendom* (Harrisburg, Pa.: Trinity Press International, 1999), p. 10. Kreider is referring to the work of Rodney Stark, *Reconstructing the Rise of Christianity: Adventures in Historical Sociology* (Princeton, N.J.: Princeton University Press, 1996), p. 8.

4 Kreider, p. 14.

5 Kreider, p. 14.

6 Ian Morgan Cron and Phil Naish, "I Want to Go Home," *Sacred Hunger* (Greenwich, Conn.: Ian Morgan Cron, 2001). Used with permission. See more about Ian Morgan Cron's music at www.iancron.com

7 Willard, p. 258.

8 Lesslie Newbigen, *The Gospel in a Pluralist Society* (Grand Rapids, Mich.: Eerdmans, 1990), pp. 222-223.

It's About a Calling—
Not a Career

I plan (according to Jesus' plan) to send Timothy to you very soon so he
can bring back all the news of you he can gather. Oh, how that will do my
heart good! I have no one quite like Timothy. He is loyal, and genuinely
concerned for you. Most people around here are looking out for themselves,
with little concern for the things of Jesus. But you know yourselves that
Timothy's the real thing.

PHILIPPIANS 2:19-22

It was one of the first conversations I (Wes) remember having with Glenn at the turn of the century. It was a few days
after he had spoken to a regional group of fellow pastors.

These "fellow pastors" were ragging on Glenn a bit, asking
him why he was staying where he was. The between-the-lines
question really was, "What's wrong with you?" An even less
subtle implication was, "You could do a lot better somewhere
else." In other words, "You could make more money and have a
larger congregation somewhere else." I'll admit, Glenn does have
more than enough capability for that.

But I continued to listen to this man's good heart. I listened
to him honestly share about tough financial times both personally
and for his congregation. Yet Glenn also told me of his great love
for the people he shepherds. Honest tears of strength and compassion welled up in his eyes as he recounted story after story
about these precious people. My heart joined his in thinking

through his intentional choices to remain where he was. I knew that it was God's choice—and God's call on his life.

What does it mean to be in pastoral ministry? Is it a calling? Or is it a career? Consider some of the differences between these two concepts.

In a career, you get to choose your direction. You map out where you're going and make choices about the next steps to further your career. You learn to care about your own self-interests and look for ways to better your situation.

A calling is quite different. In a calling, you submit to the Lord's direction. You don't get to go where you want or stay where you want. You go where the Lord clearly leads you. You stay put in difficult circumstances sometimes, even if better options or better offers come your way.

If you see pastoral ministry as a career, it makes sense to climb the ladder of success in the church business. If you're after prestige, you'll want to move on to bigger churches with better opportunities. Or if you prefer to maintain a certain standard of living while living in relative peace, you might choose to minister in a smaller church or a rural setting where the pace isn't so swift.

But if you see pastoral ministry as a calling, it makes no sense to climb the ladder of success. You'll seek to be faithful wherever the Lord puts you—in a big church or a small church, in suburbia, the inner city, or a rural setting.

If pastoral ministry is a career, then the pressure will be on to do well and to prove yourself so better offers will come your way. You'll care about how people judge your success. You'll worry about maintaining your image. You'll seek to be successful in order to become marketable. You'll write your résumé so that it presents your accomplishments and yourself in the best light.

Of course, if ministry is a calling, you'll still face pressures. But they'll be different. No longer will you need to worry about

your success or image. Instead, you'll experience pressure that comes through the cares and concerns of the church. You'll know that you're not truly in control, that you don't have all the solutions, and that some things you just can't fix. This kind of pressure, for lack of a better word, will demand that you wait on God, even when everything around you says that you're crazy to do so.

Some of our fellow pastors try to correct us and say that we're setting up a false distinction. They argue that it's not a matter of either/or—that pastoral ministry is both a calling and a career. But the distinction is clear. If ministry is a career, then you get to call the shots. If it's a calling, then you're required to be a disciple of Jesus. No one can serve two masters—especially if one of the masters is you.

The notion that pastoral ministry is both a career and a calling is not found in the New Testament. Apostles viewed themselves as bondservants of Jesus Christ and endured the worst of what the world (and the church) could give in terms of status, job security, and benefits packages. The concept of career was absent in the early church.

In addition, everyone in the church possessed a valuable ministry (see Ephesians 4 and 1 Corinthians 12). Certainly, the church had leaders, and leadership was important. But a sharp clergy/laity distinction didn't exist.

Concepts of pastoring and the role of the laity began to change during the long progression of Christendom. When Christianity became the official religion of the Roman Empire, church leadership took on an air of prestige. It's easy to see how the status of the priesthood in other cults of the empire transferred onto the leaders within the church. Church leaders developed an entire hierarchy of church leadership, modeling it after the government of the empire itself. Before long, people began

to see priests as the professional clergy, the experts, and the official interpreters of the Word of God.

Even the Reformation, with its proclamations regarding the priesthood of all believers, could not shake this deeply imbedded system. To this day, we struggle with what it means, in any practical way, for the people in the congregation to be ministers within the church.

Modernism also had an influence on pastors being seen as professionals. As the worldview of materialism and secular science replaced the Christian worldview, the church began to adopt a way to position herself in order to maintain a place in the modern world.[1] Pastors began to take on the role of instructors, therapists, and/or religious entrepreneurs in an effort to hold on to a place within society.[2]

When the biblical story is devalued, the mission of the church inevitably suffers. When the revelation of God's Word is replaced by autonomous reason, a new kind of ministry is formed—one that needs experts to interpret, teach, practice, and maintain the dogma and manage the system. Professional expertise replaces dependence on God.

The mission of the church to continue the story by proclaiming the gospel and doing the good works of the kingdom gets replaced with more suitable practices that fit more neatly into the system of modernism. Many of us have been trained to perform these functions as professionals within this system.

Let's be flat-out honest. Don't we pastors and church leaders often think that we know more than the people who sit in our pews every Sunday? After all, we've been trained in the best seminaries and Bible schools. We've studied under great scholars.

We've attended seminars and workshops. We've read the books—books that many of our church members wouldn't dare to read.

We really do think that we're the experts and that if the church is going to go somewhere, it will have to go under our leadership. Of course, when the members of our churches refuse to follow, we wonder how they dare not buy into our teaching. Who do they think they are?

But what if the Bible is right after all? What if the Holy Spirit gives his gifts not merely to the experts but instead to the whole congregation? What if the church's ministry and mission don't reside with a few select people but instead belong to everyone in the church? Doesn't this sound more like the New Testament?

Change is a scary deal for most of us. Often, it's flat-out uncomfortable. "Oh, Lord," we pray, "are we on the move again?" But if we're following the call of God on our lives, then change is inevitable and revolution necessary.[3] Inside our own hearts and within our churches, radical living for our Lord isn't a polite request. Radical, revolutionary living is expected of us.

For nearly 1,500 years we've been laboring under the Christendom model. But today we need to be a part of necessary change if we're going to be true to our Spirit-led calling as pastors of the good news of Jesus Christ.

As we're encouraged to see pastoral ministry as a calling rather than a career, we face a twofold problem. Not only do those of us within church leadership make assumptions about being the experts, but for quite a long time, we've also trained the members of our churches to think the same way. We've trained them to see us as the dispensers of knowledge, truth, vision, and ministry. We've trained them to need us instead of

each other. Their job is to come every week to receive from us. The people in the pews are the consumers of our professional services. Many are loyal customers. Some are even good friends.

In the life-squeezes of doing ministry, we no longer expect people in our congregations to be engaged in ministry or mission; we've essentially trained them to view themselves as incompetent for the task. We're the experts. It's our job. Much of church work, we've suggested, is the work of the professional staff. They're the consumers—that's their place in the system. Then we experience frustration because good workers in our churches are hard to come by.

Some of my (Wes's) favorite relatives happen to be Mormon. My wife's niece and her family are our favorites, not because they're Mormon, but because we love them for who they are—and I think they love us for the same reason. In a recent conversation, my wife was surprised to find out that the Mormon church exists at the local level, operating almost exclusively by lay people. They have a radical understanding of their personal parts in their local ward and how they fit in with the Mormon church as a whole, all the way to the top in Salt Lake City. Granted, we have some significant differences of belief with these dear people, but I'm amazed by and genuinely respect the fact that they have no paid church staff and that the people are called—even required—to do the work of their church.

How sad that we Christian pastors, instead of equipping people for ministry, have too often asked them to merely buy our religious services and products, finance our plans, and cheer us on. By doing so, we've gladly accepted our role as professional practitioners.

We've set ourselves up: Now we have to prove that we know what we're doing. Success in terms of church growth becomes a necessity. Now the church must become more like a business

with manageable and measurable growth. Unless it succeeds, the "stockholders" will have to hire a new CEO to lead the church to its glory days. Too many pastors have crumbled under the pressure and weight of this system.

One book we've mentioned, *In the Name of Jesus: Reflections on Christian Leadership,*[4] doesn't provide formulas or gimmicks. Instead, the author, Henri Nouwen, causes us to consider the temptations of being relevant, spectacular, and powerful—the same temptations Satan presented to Jesus. We all suffer from those temptations. Nouwen simply yet powerfully helps us think through our responses and invites us to return to our calling.

Reflecting on Nouwen's words makes us realize that most of the time we pastors largely don't know what we're doing. We really aren't the experts after all. We've simply allowed ourselves to be positioned this way in a flawed system that has been coming at us for a long, long time.

If you're totally honest about your ministry, would you admit that you feel way in over your head a lot of the time? Do you often feel alone? That's why we must learn again and again, with freshness and vitality, to walk by faith. Our calling as pastors is way beyond us because it's spiritual in nature. We need to stop being the experts and start pointing our people to the Sovereign God who alone knows the end and the beginning.

Instead of trusting us, our congregants must learn to trust in him. Instead of following us, they must follow him. Instead of trusting in our own capabilities and great ideas, our educations, or the latest formulas for success, we too must learn to rest in and follow God more fully and completely into what he's calling us to be and do.

Nudging back to the much older ways—the ways of the "ancient/future"—isn't going to be easy. If ministry is a calling, then our focus needs to be a lot different. It may even cost us our present identity.

Let's face it: Much of our identity has to do with what we think are important measures of church work: attendance, money, successful programs, and facilities. Our congregations have learned to measure our success the same way. We've all grown comfortable with this business view of the church. We've learned to protect our careers in order to move up the corporate ladder in the church business. All of this places enormous pressure on us to succeed.

But what if ministry really is still a calling instead of a career? What if success, in the ways that we've measured it, doesn't really matter? What if we can get our whole church to buy into the much older, apostolic way of looking at ministry? Won't this take off the pressure?

Instead of demanding the blessings of God on our ministries, let's seek out and learn renewed ways to trust God. We can accept by faith that God is still at work—even when things don't go the way we plan. We can labor with a different intensity—one that rests on faith rather than accomplishments. We can again see how we fit into the story of God's redemption—a story in which we get to write a chapter or two because of his calling on our lives.

A good business friend of ours works with clients to help them ascend to their calling in life, whether in the "ministry place" or the marketplace. That's an admirable goal! No matter what side of the pulpit we're on, are we ascending to our calling? Are we

in a place where we can serve God most fully through how he has wired, created, and gifted us? As pastors, are we helping those we lead and influence to ascend to their calling both inside and outside the church?

We need to rediscover the concept of calling. In our churches, and in the smaller communities within our churches, we need to help each other ascend to our calling.[5] The concept of calling will keep us humble and dependent on God. It will help us find our identity where it belongs, as children of our heavenly Father—children who are grateful for the calling of being appointed to his service.

Rediscovering the concept of calling will give us the emotional, spiritual, and moral toughness we need to get through the days ahead. We can again revel in God's grace rather than our own works. We might also learn to agonize over the things that break our Father's heart rather than despair over our own disappointments and failures.

A renewed concept of calling will require us to give up ownership of the ministry. It will mean giving up our dreams, plans, and expectations to listen instead to God's commands. It will mean focusing again on God's Word and sharing more of our Father's heart. It will require us to be faithful.

We love the verses from Philippians that started this discussion on calling versus career. Here they are from the *New International Version:* "I hope in the Lord Jesus to send Timothy to you soon, that I also may be cheered when I receive news about you. I have no one else like him, who takes a genuine interest in your welfare. For everyone looks out for his own interests, not those of Jesus Christ. But you know that Timothy has proved himself" (2:19-22).

These words demonstrate what it means to be engaged in the calling. As a pastor, you're called to have a genuine interest in the

welfare of your flock. You don't need to concern yourself with what you can get out of them or what they can do to strengthen your agenda. They don't serve your interests. Together you share your hearts to seek after God's will. You learn to listen to one another to hear what the Spirit is saying to your church.

Even more interesting is the comment that Paul makes about everyone looking out for his or her own interests rather than the interests of Christ. To be engaged in the calling means to die to our own interests and center our energy on Christ's interests. It's not about climbing a ladder of success or seeking to further our careers.

As pastors, we must follow Jesus. We must be desperate disciples that first gain direction in life from him before we go out to influence others to do the same. We must be persons of faith and conviction in the place where the Lord has called us. We can no longer be seen as experts or professionals. Instead, we must call the sheep to follow us as we follow Jesus.

Seeing ministry as a calling doesn't mean the road ahead will be uncomplicated. We'll be groping our way forward. We need to listen to one another as we treat everyone in the body of Christ with kindness and respect. We need to equip all the saints for ministry and refuse to be the answer person.

Walking by faith isn't a simple matter. It requires us to realize that we don't have all the answers. It demands a certain and significant tolerance for the unknown. We must learn anew to walk by faith. Someone has said that hope is faith holding out its hand in the dark. What are you reaching out to as you stumble forward in God's direction?

Going forward to the much older ways won't be an easy task. The concept of career—of professional ministry—is deeply

imbedded within us. Some of us would rather not go forward because we're comfortable where we are. We like being seen as the experts. Our people are comfortable with this system as well. They don't mind being consumers. The cost of being a consumer isn't nearly as steep as the cost of discipleship.

Yet sooner or later, we must all bow our hearts before God. What will he say to us about how we've lived out the calling he placed on our lives before the world began? Will he look into our eyes and say, "Well done"?

The central question is,

Are the leaders of the future truly men and women of God, people with an ardent desire to dwell in God's presence, to listen to God's voice, to look at God's beauty, to touch God's incarnate Word and to taste fully God's infinite goodness?[6]

---

[1] For a more complete discussion of these ideas, see Alan J. Roxburgh, *The Missionary Congregation, Leadership, and Liminality* (Harrisburg, Pa.: Trinity Press International, 1997), pp. 15-22.

[2] Two books by Brian McLaren of significant value to read are *A New Kind of Christian: A Tale of Two Friends on a Spiritual Journey* (San Francisco: Jossey-Bass, 2001), especially chapter 2 as it relates to how we got to where we are in the current church, and *The Story We Find Ourselves In: Further Adventures of a New Kind of Christian* (San Francisco: Jossey-Bass, 2003).

[3] See Dwight Edwards, *Revolution Within: A Fresh Look at Supernatural Living* (Colorado Springs, Colo.: WaterBrook Press, 2001).

[4] We encourage you to read Nouwen's *In the Name of Jesus* (Crossroad, 1998) at least once a year.

[5] We suggest you browse through Dr. Larry Crabb's website, www.newwayministries.org, which offers exceptional opportunities to change and grow within your own life and the life of your church.

[6] Nouwen, pp. 29-30.

It's About Character—
Not Credentials

If anyone wants to provide leadership in the church, good! But there are preconditions: A leader must be well-thought-of, committed to his wife, cool and collected, accessible, and hospitable. He must know what he's talking about, not be overfond of wine, not pushy but gentle, not thin-skinned, not money-hungry. He must handle his own affairs well, attentive to his own children and having their respect.

1 Timothy 3:1-4

It might surprise you to learn that the apostle Peter, Polycarp, Athanasius, St. Augustine, John Calvin, and Charles Spurgeon didn't have seminary degrees. Neither does Bill Hybels. Joseph Ricci doesn't have one either.

Toward the end of 2002, I (Glenn) had breakfast with Joe. Joe has a rare, progressive neurological disease. This disease is so rare that it doesn't have a name yet. As Joe sat in his wheelchair, I cut his eggs and he told his story.

Not long after Joe came to faith in Christ, he sensed that he wanted to serve the Lord. As he put it, "Not to pay him back, just to serve him." So he asked his pastor if he could get involved in some ministry. Joe was suffering physically with his disability, and on the surface it seemed he might not be able to do much.

But Joe's pastor responded to his request by offering him a tape-duplicating machine. The pastor had rigged a recording device in the pulpit and used it to tape his sermons for a few

shut-ins who couldn't come to worship. He dropped the dupli-cator off at Joe's house and asked him if he would copy and deliver the tapes.

Joe quickly realized that he could use the duplicator for other purposes. Before long, he was also duplicating Bible study teach-ers' lessons and conference speakers' lectures and distributing these tapes. In a few years, Joe ran out of room for this ministry in his home, so he approached his pastor about setting up shop in a room in the church building. The church council was amenable to Joe's request, so he took over a room.

Later, as Joe faithfully ministered with his tapes, one of the leaders in the church approached him about the position of property manager for the congregation. While Joe was unable to do any of the physical labor, he could oversee the work and make certain it was done properly. After praying about this new opportunity for service, Joe accepted the position, while at the same time continuing with his tape ministry.

Because of his new position, Joe requested that a phone be installed in his office at the church so he could stay on top of managing the church property. The church provided the phone, and soon Joe was answering calls—often referring people to other church leaders or the church staff.

Interestingly, sometimes no one was available except Joe. Soon he was receiving calls from people in spiritual and emo-tional need. He found himself in the position of giving spiritual guidance and praying with people over the phone.

As time moved on, the people in leadership recognized Joe's gifts. Though retired and disabled, Joe enjoys a thriving ministry of helps and encouragement at Our Savior's Lutheran Church just outside Albany, New York. At the time I visited with him, Joe was meeting with people four days a week, and for several years he has hosted a weekly call-in program on

WHAZ, the local Christian radio station.

Joe has no formal training. He has no seminary degree. But Joe is a disciple of Christ. He has character and a special gifting from the Holy Spirit.

The accumulation of titles, credentials, and degrees has become very important within church as we know it today. It has become a way of proving an expertise for doing church work and bolstering a career in ministry.

With the right degrees and titles, we can move up the ladder in the church business. We use titles to claim our official status as church leaders or to bolster our self-image. They maintain our professionalism. But we're not called to professionalism; we're called to sacrificial service.

Giving honor and being thankful for the accomplishment of educational pursuits is fine. The respect we get when someone calls us "pastor" feels good. But when we're tending our lost and hurting sheep, titles don't really matter. Relationships always do. Too often titles don't encourage relationships or the growth and development of character in ourselves or the people we serve.

Many denominations and church fellowships sorrowfully overemphasize degrees from a seminary as the "ordinary" path to ordination. We know of one man who was very qualified from his heart and life experience, yet he was turned down for an important position in a new church because he lacked the "right" education. What have we done to ourselves?

Thankfully, some church associations at least have an "extraordinary" clause in their governing documents to allow people who're aren't formally and academically educated, but who are wise and full of God's character, to be ordained.

Perhaps as we move into the future, the extraordinary clause will become more ordinary.

Just so you don't jump to poor conclusions, we do want to acknowledge the great value formal education can have. I (Glenn) offer much thanks for my years of education. During those years, I established a theological foundation and gathered useful tools for interpreting Scripture that I still use today. Some of this study was done with outstanding biblical scholars whom God used to shape and change my life for the better.

Formal education certainly has value, but some important questions loom large. Does formal education really prepare you for real relationships and authentic, life-transforming living? Does the knowledge you gain challenge you to be a lifelong learner, or are you satisfied with what you know? Does your education propel you to first and foremost be a servant of the Most High King?

Do we really think that titles and degrees mean anything to God? Or are we willing to snuggle in close to his Spirit and revel in the fact that he calls us "friend," "my son," or "my daughter"? What else do we really need?

When we go back to the Bible, we don't find any formal education requirements for ministry. What we do find are other requirements having to do with character. The old ways of Christendom made these character requirements secondary.

Character has to do with your quality as a person—who you are, even when no one else is looking. Jesus often took the Pharisees to task because of their hypocrisy (see Matthew 23). The Pharisees made a pretense of religion. They were faking it. They hid behind a façade of religion quite different from their inward natures. Character is a matter of integrity.

Delightedly, my wife and I (Wes) sat in a church in the Seattle area in June 2003 as one of our closest friends was honored for his ten years of service as senior pastor. At a point in the lively and heart-warming presentations of gratitude, his wife took the microphone and thanked the congregation for all their care and assured them that this man was the "real deal"—that he was the same at home as in front of them. From my thirty years of friendship with this man, I know his wife's claim is true.

Character is more critical than ever in God's work. Sadly, the whole world has been questioning character recently as news headlines scream of instances when many clergy and other church leaders have easily ignored character. We cringe a bit as we recall the scandals of the popes and priests at the height of the Christendom period. Even to this day, the church is plagued with men and women who don't do well in meeting the character requirements for ministry, although they certainly have the credentials.

The character requirements in 1 Timothy 3:2-7 include such qualities as having self-control in all facets of our lives and being temperate, respectable within our communities and at home, hospitable, not violent but gentle, not quarrelsome, and not a lover of money. Second Timothy 2:24 says that the Lord's servant must be kind to everyone, able to teach, and not resentful.

We've all heard about—or been part of—church association meetings, presbytery meetings, or church elder or deacon meetings where well-meaning people wrangled over carpet and paint colors or some regulatory principle concerning worship (do we sing just hymns or do we do "church karaoke"—you know, following the bouncing ball over the words on a big screen?). Too often, these battles take us away from the main task of shepherding and nurturing people.

While we make light of these things, sometimes they can be

important. Our point is this: Can't we discuss these matters—and even deeper and more important matters—with respect, self-control and gentleness, and some occasional good humor? What happened to our Christian character—the character required for pastoral office in the church?

We've all seen people in ministry who seem to love to fight, who chase after money, and who love self-indulgence. Somehow we've too often yielded to the tendency toward professionalism and have become blinded to the character requirements of a New Testament leader.

Our character is who we are. It shows through any pretenses we have. We can try to hide our character by building up a false image, often using our degrees and credentials to do so. But sooner or later our character bleeds through. We can't hide it forever.

Consider for a moment what we know about the early, apostolic model for the church. Take a look at the disciples Jesus chose. What a motley crew they were! Dirty, smelly fishermen. A tax collector. Not the kind of people we'd put in charge of the church. They had no formal education, no degrees, no credentials. They had only one claim for their authority—they'd been with Jesus.

Their relationship with Jesus changed their lives. It gave them character. On this foundation, the church began. These weren't perfect men. The women who surrounded Jesus weren't perfect either. Far from it! But being with him changed them forever. Oh, that we'd pray for and realize the same for our own lives.

The people who followed Jesus were people of character—so much so that these anointed and appointed leaders could urge others to follow their own example in following the Lord. Their

changed lives were the fuel that powered the expansion of the church in its earliest days. By following their example of Christian character, the early church exploded into existence.

How are you being changed by having Jesus in your life? What happens to the people who follow you in your ministries? Listen to Paul, as he wrote to those he loved in Phillipi:

> Summing it all up, friends, I'd say you'll do best by filling your minds and meditating on things true, noble, reputable, authentic, compelling, gracious—the best, not the worst; the beautiful, not the ugly; things to praise, not things to curse. Put into practice what you learned from me, what you heard and saw and realized. Do that, and God, who makes everything work together, will work you into his most excellent harmonies. (Philippians 4:8-9)

If we long to encounter such growth in our day, the secret isn't in some magic or science of church growth. Instead, Christian character matters more, especially among the leaders of the church.

The reality of our Christianity, authentically lived out in our relationships and deepening our communities, will make the larger difference in our postmodern world. People need more than window dressing or image. They need, as Wes's good friend expressed it, "the real deal."

Consider for yourself: Do people take note of the fact that you've been with Jesus? Are they able to tell that you've been changed by your relationship with the living Lord? Is your character consistent with the calling you've received from the Lord?

God knows your heart. And so do those who are consistently around you.

We come to you with a plea for all of us in pastoral ministry. We're asking these questions of ourselves as well as you: What are you doing to deal with your own heart before God? Is your heart genuinely open before the Lord? Where are you hiding even petty sins, let alone any "big ones"? Are you putting more emphasis on dealing with your heart than on trying to protect your image?

Part of this plea we've taken from Acts 20:28: *"Keep watch over yourselves* and all the flock of which the Holy Spirit has made you overseers" (NIV, emphasis added). If we own up to the truth, many of us are too busy and too consumed with doing the "stuff" of church business to spend adequate time doing what is necessary to take care of ourselves and our flock. We're too busy for times of prayer, quiet, reflection, and solitude. But how else will we develop the godly character we need to serve the flock?

Consider how Eugene Peterson brought insight to 1 Timothy 2:1-3 in *The Message*. In this passage, Paul (an old man) was writing a personal letter to Timothy (a young man) concerning the "first things first" about being a healthy church leader:

> The first thing I want you to do is pray. Pray every way you know how, for everyone you know. Pray especially for rulers and their governments to rule well so we can be quietly about our business of living simply, in humble contemplation. This is the way our Savior God wants us to live.

In this day and age, that sounds almost impossible. But God wouldn't put it in his Word if it weren't possible. "The first thing I want you to do is pray." Can you imagine what could happen

in and through us if we actually took this one sentence seriously? We'd be thoroughly amazed if, through prayer, we unleashed God's grace in our lives and in our congregations.

As we move into the future, we need to recapture these character requirements that Scripture lays down for us. The mission of God depends on it.

The unchurched don't care much about our credentials. Bible school and seminary degrees aren't important if we can't undergird them with our wholehearted response to God's character requirements. We must live out the reality of our message. And we live it out best in community and relationships when we deeply share our lives, our dreams, our joys, and our sorrows.

What people expect of us—their pastors and church leaders—is that we be holy men and women, that we love justice and mercy, that we sacrifice ourselves for the sake of the sheep, including sheep that are lost. They want to know that their pastors aren't always looking for a fight or motivated by money. They long for leaders who are patient and gentle, kind and generous—pastors who love them.

Only from this foundation do we have the right to speak the truth into people's lives. As pastors, we sometimes must say dreadfully truthful things to people. But we must do so with gentleness. We once heard that sacred process explained this way: "It was like he opened my chest and took out my heart and did heart surgery. Then he placed my heart back into my chest, and I never felt a thing."

Now that's gentleness! May we develop such genuine gentleness as we deal with people concerning difficult matters. It's what Jesus did for the children—and for any lost sheep. Jesus wants to do the same through us, through our character.

One more thought. As we consider the ordination process many pastors go through to affirm their calling to ministry, let's put the character issue up front. Let's ask character questions first. What does the candidate believe about money? What kind of up-close, long-term interpersonal relationships does he have? Who are her best friends and for how long have they been friends? What kind of healthy relationships does he enjoy with others in ministry? Does she have broken or strained relationships, and if so, what's she doing about them? How does he get along with his spouse? How does she manage and encourage her family? In what ways is he respectful, hospitable, and self-controlled? What personal and intimate community or small group is she part of and submitted to—totally known by, warts and all?

Let's also ask more questions about the candidate's personal life, past and present. How does he realistically assess his strengths and not-so-strong points? What are her desires for the future? In what ways is he a person of prayer? How much time does she spend meditating on Scripture? Does he have integrity? In what situations is her heart sincerely broken concerning spiritual issues in people's lives?

After we've examined the candidate's character, then we can look at areas of doctrine, Bible knowledge, church history, and so forth that education provides. Let's not worry so much about whether the candidate has the degree. Let's be more concerned with the heart and commitment to relationships. Let's ask if this person is gifted for pastoral ministry, considering character first.

Months back, I (Wes) had dinner with a deep and creative pastor and his associate pastor. These men have a radical vision of how to prepare other leaders for the church. Both of these men graduated from two different well-known and well-respected seminaries. But they also have come to grips with the fact that something continues to be desperately missing from

most leadership programs. So with the full approval of their elders, they're creating a small training school for future church leaders. Character will be addressed head-on, growing out of Bible teaching and doctrinal studies.

These men know they don't have all the answers. But they're passionate—even on fire—about the fact that something needs to change, beginning with how they develop church leaders within their own small congregation.[1]

What they propose for their training school is fresh and radical. Academics will be strong. Biblical literacy will be crucial. But developing character, community, and relationships will be even more important. Who knows, they may just change the life of some fisherman or an ex-IRS worker who will lead the church to a new frontier—just like Jesus did.

---

[1] One of the most important books we've read in recent years is Robert E. Webber, *The Younger Evangelicals: Facing the Challenges of the New World* (Grand Rapids, Mich.: Baker, 2002). His excellent research and conversations with many younger and younger-at-heart church leaders provide critical reading for those of us who desire to be a part of the church in the future.

It's About Community— Not Just Management

All the believers lived in a wonderful harmony, holding everything in common. They sold whatever they owned and pooled their resources so that each person's need was met. They followed a daily discipline of worship in the Temple followed by meals at home, every meal a celebration, exuberant and joyful, as they praised God.

ACTS 2:44-47

Community is more than a village or town. In church circles, it's more than a small group. Not to titillate your curiosity, but we know some larger-than-life, well-known names in current Christianity who've expressed that community is hard to come by for them. It's hard to trust a group of people, to find a safe place.

The well-known aren't the only ones suffering from lack of honest, authentic, safe, trustworthy community. The events of September 11, 2001, jolted us into the realization that we need people who know us deeply in the strong and not-so-strong places in our lives. We can't do this "Christian" thing in isolation. Even the Trinity is a community—the *original* community.

At his Soul Care conferences, Larry Crabb points out that the best of community takes place in an intentional small group focusing on spiritual formation. He notes that this kind of intentional community is *not* simply

- a Bible study,
- a prayer meeting,
- a support group,
- a catch-up-on-each-other's-lives group, or
- a social group.

Crabb *does* define this kind of intentional community as a handful of Jesus-followers who

- grasp the essentials of New Covenant Theology,
- recognize the gospel's provisions for enjoying God as our supreme treasure,
- commit themselves to First-Things—to living the New Way,
- long more than anything else to know God and to become like Christ through the Spirit,
- see the crucial role of relationships in spiritual formation, being so desperate to know God that the risk of vulnerability is worth the cost, and
- covenant together to become agents of spiritual formation in each other's lives.[1]

Interestingly, we regularly hear people say that they don't experience much of the above in their small groups. Hearing this hunger for community in their hearts is both surprising and encouraging. And it's evidence that we need to be doing some things very differently in our churches when it comes to community—no matter what size our church gathering may be.

Robert Webber supports this thought in his exceptional book, *The Younger Evangelicals.* Webber, close to seventy (yet very young in heart), has done an outstanding job of giving us a look at the last hundred years of evangelicalism, focusing even more

closely on the last fifty years. He has listened well to those who will be leading the church now and in the future. He quotes five vibrant younger leaders:

> John Green, founder of a ministry to gay and lesbian street prostitutes in Chicago writes, "The Christian church is so enmeshed with the American culture that it cannot see that the same culture is frighteningly anti-Christian. . . . We are made to be a light in the darkness—calling people to the road less traveled, to a costly discipleship that rejects the materialism, nationalism, militarism, classism, racism, and sexism of the American culture for the cross of Christ."
>
> Green points to the "ecclesial community of premodern and postmodern times as an alternative community, a contrast culture and society of people." He writes, "The church is not called to be a business marketing itself to meet the needs of consumers who wrongly believe they know exactly what they need. Instead, the church is family." This family "is intended to be a local and organic garden planted in the soil of a greater community and as such is rooted in that time and place."
>
> The younger evangelical is interested in building organic Christian community, not huge Wal-Mart churches that deliver a full range of Christian consumer goods. Steve Ibbotson, who teaches at Prairie Bible College, believes postmoderns have "an incredible thirst for real community, real love and care." This is why, as Tory Baucum, a young professor at Asbury Seminary, says, "We honeycomb the parish with small groups (of all kinds) and create a culture of honest conversation."

Church isn't just a "Sunday morning experience." Instead, as Mark Driscoll writes, "It is a family with members of all ages . . . a family with members who are students and software designers and retail clerks and parents and construction workers . . . a family with members who have an intimate relationship with God, others who desire to know him better and still others who don't know him at all . . . a family who gathers to worship God, to pray, to learn, and for some to just hang out."

Dieter Zander, a younger evangelical church planter in San Francisco, was hired to begin a Generation X church within Willow Creek Community Church near Chicago but was uneasy with the "church within a church" approach. This younger generation wants the wisdom of other generations; they don't want to be separated out as a group with the characteristics they "will grow out of and graduate from." Instead, writes Zander, Xers have "the very characteristics that the church ought to grow into," one of them being their commitment to the intergenerational church, another their love of intercultural communities.[2]

Based on these thoughts, we'd like to add to the definition of community: Community includes the bonding of uncommon people around a common mission. This happens in a way that the needs of the group have a higher priority than one's individual needs. This is why Paul encouraged Bithynians, Greeks, Jews, Gentiles, males, females, slaves, and the free who acknowledged Jesus as Lord and Savior to live together in loving, authentic relationships (see Galatians 3:26-29; Ephesians 4:1-6; Colossians 3:11-15).

Community is vitally important because the church—the community of God's people—is the hermeneutic of the gospel. In other words, the community of the church is the living, breathing, in-your-face demonstration of what it means to live under the reign of God.

As a community, we're called to make sense of the gospel to the watching world. When people want to know what it's like to live under the reign of God, they ought to be able to point to the Christian community and say, "That's what it's like." How we live with one another and relate to the rest of the world is crucial to the purposes of the kingdom of God.

Even a cursory walk through the pages of the Bible demonstrates the importance of community. Just as God exists in community in the mystery of the Trinity, we were created for community. Doesn't your soul long for that?

The book of Genesis tells us how God chose Abraham to be a man of faith and to raise up a community. The pages of the Old Testament move on to show us how this community came into being. The people of God were called to live in community as a holy nation so that others would see their distinction and come to know their God.

Within the pages of the New Testament we see the church become the new community called to minister the good news of the kingdom to the world by word and deed. Notice that our calling to minister the gospel to the world is a matter that flows from our community as God's people.

> You [plural] are the salt of the earth. . . . You [plural] are the light of the world. . . . No one has ever seen God; but if we love one another, God lives in us [plural] and his love is made complete in us. (Matthew 5:13-14, NIV; 1 John 4:12, NIV, emphasis added)

Sadly, many local congregations have lost much of the sense of their corporate witness. They've forgotten that they're *corporately* the agent and sign and foretaste of the kingdom.[3] How we live and deal with one another in community directly relates to our witness to the world. Jesus said, "This is how everyone will recognize that you are my disciples—when they see the love you have for each other" (John 13:35).

In our day, isn't it difficult to believe that statement? After all, we have a large menu of new and insightful techniques for growing the church. We have great productions, slick marketing procedures, and so much more technology at our disposal. We've learned useful managerial methods that have (at least in some contexts) proven to be instrumental to the success of the church. So to call people to community—to intentionally care for one another and share our burdens and joys with one another— seems a bit archaic in light of all this success. Yet unless someone changed the New Testament without us knowing, God still calls us to community—to intentional spiritual formation as we open up to each other and thus to our triune God.

With a few exceptions, we live in a culture that has immersed itself in the value of individualism. It's pervasive. It's hard to admit that we're needy. We expect people to get on with their lives without being a bother to anyone, and we place the same expectation on ourselves.

Instead of building community, we pretend to be what we're not. We claim to be "just fine." But inside we're aching, and we don't know where to take that ache. We don't own up to our weaknesses very well. In the midst of all this delusion, the church focuses on management techniques to appeal to individ-

uals and manipulate them into some kind of cohesion—a cohesion that never threatens their individual rights or deals with any issues of the heart. The concept of a corporate, covenant people of God has been replaced by individualism. We've lost the concept of community.

Of course, pockets of believers stumble into community through small groups or in smaller churches. Since 2001, my wife, Judy, and I (Wes) have finally been experiencing community at its richest depths. After a long journey, we've found a group of four couples (ourselves included) that's unlike anything else we've experienced. Even as people in our fifties and sixties, we've had to abandon old ways to embrace the much older ways of community we'd only dreamed about in all our years of "Christian experience."

Church has become optional for many people. And why not? If people focus on themselves and their individual needs, who needs a church? By buying into the ideals of individualism, we've fostered a Lone Ranger mentality within the church.

You can see this in the way we try to reach the unchurched. We appeal to people on the basis of their individual needs. The experts encourage us to make our programming like a mall or a cafeteria, offering a multiplicity of services to meet multiple individual needs.

We also orchestrate the programs of our churches to meet the felt needs of individual consumers. Children get their needs met in one place, adolescents are catered to in another, and adults find still other programs for their needs. By doing this, the church aids in the fragmentation of community. Of course, meeting needs *is* important, but the church has far greater priorities.

Not only has modernism led to individualism, making us independent and self-reliant, but it has also impressed upon us the value of pragmatism. In other words, if it works—no matter

what it is—it's good. Does community work? That's probably what some of you are asking at this point. Such a question demonstrates how far down the road we've traveled from our roots in the early church.

The chief concern of the early church was not a matter of doing "what works" but a matter of being the people of God. Much of the skewed perspective we have today has to do with our confusion on this issue. We concentrate so much effort on *growing* the church that we spend little or no effort on *being* the church.

Hear this loud and clear: Principles of management to encourage organization are not out of line in our society. Too many churches are a bit sloppy in their legal and organizational procedures. But management principles shouldn't supplant the faith and trust and fellowship we're called to live out daily in our church communities. What happens between people in community needs to be a higher priority than organization.[4]

In order to demonstrate to what degree we have replaced biblical thinking with management principles (and how much these principles have shifted us away from being the church), let's briefly look at just one of the unquestioned truths of the church-growth movement: the homogeneous unit principle. As commonly understood, this principle teaches that churches tend to attract people who are similar to their current members. Churches determine who their "target audience" is for church growth, and then they seek to attract people in their vicinity who are "just like them."

This is why churches of predominantly black members attract black people and churches of predominantly white members attract white people. Churches made up mostly of young married couples attract people in that social category, and churches made up of families attract more family people. We're told that this is one of the laws of church growth because it explains how churches grow.

We've seen churches program their events and services around the homogeneous unit principle. Many times, this centers on the style of worship services offered. A certain style supposedly appeals to Gen Xers, and it's different from what boomers appreciate. Seniors prefer yet a different style of worship. Pastors have even planted churches with a certain generational target in mind.

The homogeneous unit principle does seem to work. It explains why many churches are growing. We're thankful that God uses these churches to draw people to himself. Still, the principle itself seems detrimental to the church's nature. The very nature of the church isn't about a homogeneous unit—whether social, economic, age, or gender. The nature of the church—and the way we demonstrate kingdom living to the rest of the world—is about breaking down these social norms so that all may be one in Christ.

The people in my (Glenn's) smaller church in New Jersey love to sing the song "Break Dividing Walls." The chorus speaks of the unity that we have in the faith, despite our racial backgrounds, economic differences, or church traditions. I think this ragamuffin band of Christ-followers (and aren't we all ragamuffins when we stand before our Lord?) could sing this song every Sunday. My church loves this true expression of our hearts as a congregation.

Somehow the saints at my church have grasped the idea that the multifaceted, multigenerational, and multiethnic kingdom of God is a beautiful thing that they should not only enjoy but also celebrate. This is the nature of the church where "there is neither Jew nor Greek, slave nor free, male nor female, for you are all one in Christ Jesus" (Galatians 3:28, NIV).

Our hope is to somehow persuade you that what really matters in terms of our witness to the world is focusing on the very nature of the church. That seems to be what Jesus told us to do. Let's be the church of God's original intent, with a high emphasis on community.

These words bring a certain sense of apprehension to us. We've lived our lives under a worldview that preaches individualism. Most of us could agree with the statement, "I want to live my own life, chart my own course, and rule my own destiny." We're told that these things are our rights as individuals.

To move beyond this mentality, we have to make a conscious effort to think in terms of community, to listen to the deep-down longings of our hearts. We have to press our understanding of Scripture in this area to see and understand what God's Word truly says.

Encouraging authentic community isn't going to be easy. Building community means thinking about the needs of others before we think about ourselves. It means learning to appreciate the discomfort of being with people who aren't like us. It means learning personal sacrifice. It means setting aside time in our already crammed schedules to "waste our time" with other people who will cramp our styles and who don't care about our personal agendas.

In *An Unstoppable Force,* Erwin McManus writes from the experience of the church he leads in Los Angeles. The name of the church is simply Mosaic, and it's an intercultural, intergenerational community of believers. Consider these thoughts from the introduction of his book as he contemplates where the church has come from and where we need to be heading:

> Pastors [in the past] were valued for their ability to
> bring and keep order rather than for their ability to

bring and lead change. The reality was that pastors were being equipped to preserve the past rather than to create the future. We became known for being traditional rather than transformational. The ritual replaced the radical. The pastor/teacher replaced the apostle/evangelist.

The Church soon lost her momentum and had less and less to manage. Seminaries were producing pastors who were ready for their pulpits but not for the challenge. Pastors found themselves experts in biblical exegesis, but novices on cultural exegesis. The rapid shifts in society only added to their dilemma. We knew something was wrong, but we couldn't quite place it. America was turning from a Christian-friendly nation to, at best, Christian-indifferent. The playing field was definitely changing, and we were unprepared for the new rules.

In many ways the emergence of the parachurch reflects the paralysis within the local church. When we stopped calling youth to the mission of Christ, Youth With A Mission emerged. When we ignored the opportunity to reach university students, Campus Crusade emerged. When we settled for church attendance and neglected discipleship, Navigators emerged. When we hesitated to call men to the role of spiritual leadership, Promise Keepers emerged. Yet while the parachurch was rallying and mobilizing men and women whose hearts were longing to serve Christ, it was at the same time accelerating the spiritual anemia and decline of the local church. The church became a fortress from the world rather than the hope of the world. This disconnection from our present context exemplifies the need for holistic ministry. Seekers are looking for spiritual

integration. This means we must provide community with cause and meaning with healing. Having one without the other only leaves us fragmented. We must transform the fragments into a mosaic.[5]

Learning to live in community calls each of us to die to ourselves for the sake of our brothers and sisters in Christ. Not only must we learn to live this way as an example to our flocks, but we must also challenge and encourage others to do the same.

Let's face it: These aren't appealing messages that will draw great numbers to our churches. In fact, they'll likely do just the opposite. I (Glenn) have had younger people leave our church because they wanted more specified programs for themselves or their children. I've had older people complain because they thought the younger people were calling the shots. And I've had to respond negatively to calls from people shopping for programs of their own special interest that our church doesn't offer.

But the people who remain in our small church gladly meet for worship and sing "Break Dividing Walls" together because they instinctively know the rightness of what they are doing. They *are* the people of God—people called to give up their own rights and privileges for the sake of community, people beginning to understand that community is a greater goal than their own individual needs. When this happens, they sense something greater than themselves at work. And there is. This is possible for your church, too.

In the short run, building community isn't going to put your church on the list of the top-ten growing churches. But in the long run, it will begin to pay greater dividends than you can even dream of right now.

Imagine a church where people learn to be tolerant and patient with one another, to be givers rather than takers. Isn't this what it

means to make disciples? How can we make disciples if we're not willing to deny ourselves and follow the example of Jesus?

The communities that we foster within the church will spill out into our local communities. The church will proclaim the good news of the kingdom by its very existence—as a community, in contrast to an individualistic culture. We'll demonstrate to our local communities that we accept one another and care for each other because Jesus Christ is Lord. And that we *always* have room for more to be part of our communities.

Sooner or later, people will tire of the consumerism and individualism that drive much of our current church culture. They won't somehow mysteriously lose their selfishness. But eventually, they'll look for something deeper that can only be found in community.

People are already growing tired of phoniness. They long for an authentic community of faith. When you eat junk food for a few weeks, it's a relief to sit down to a real, nourishing, satisfying meal.

Not only does individualism break down our relationships with one another, but it also gives us a misunderstanding of who we are in the story of God's redemption. The church of today barely comprehends that we stand in a long line with people who have gone before us. We don't see our calling to continue their work. In Hebrews 11, we read about a long list of saints from the past that concludes with our connection to them: "Not one of these people, even though their lives of faith were exemplary, got their

hands on what was promised. God had a better plan for us: that their faith and our faith would come together to make one completed whole, their lives of faith not complete apart from ours" (39-40).

It's amazing to think that the work of Abraham and Moses, David and Samuel is incomplete apart from what we do today. But that's what the writer of Hebrews is telling us. The story is still being written. We, together with all of God's people, are a part of the story of God's great plan of salvation for the world. The story will continue to be written until the Lord returns.

This really is a whole lot bigger than we are—bigger than our individual needs. This is about God's purposes and plans for his world. These plans are only accomplished in the community of the saints when we subordinate our own individual desires, dreams, and needs around a common purpose that's far bigger than anything we are individually.

And we benefit, because the community of the church can be powerful. It can bring healing. It can set people free from bondage. It can give encouragement and bind up the broken-hearted. Nothing is so special about us as individuals, but God has given his Spirit to the community of the church. God speaks to us about community in Ephesians 2:19-22:

> You're no longer wandering exiles. This kingdom of
> faith is now your home country. You're no longer
> strangers or outsiders. You *belong* here, with as much
> right to the name Christian as anyone. God is building a
> home. He's using us all—irrespective of how we got
> here—in what he is building. He used the apostles and
> prophets for the foundation. Now he's using you, fitting
> you in brick by brick, stone by stone, with Christ Jesus
> as the cornerstone that holds all the parts together. We

see it taking shape day after day—a holy temple built by God, all of us built into it, a temple in which God is quite at home.

The Bible tells us that the ascended Jesus has sent his Spirit to the church, that the community of the church is the temple of the Holy Spirit, and that the Spirit gives gifts to the church for our mutual edification. What distinguishes us from all the other institutions on earth is the fact that we're a community of the Holy Spirit.

Realizing that we're in essence a Holy-Spiritual community should again make us cautious about the usefulness and relevance of using business and management techniques to achieve success within the church. Certainly, order is important. Crowds can be gathered. We can launch new programs. Raising money is important. Nothing is wrong with building or remodeling facilities. But in the midst of all this busyness, is anyone becoming a disciple of Jesus? Is spiritual transformation taking place? Are people experiencing change of character? Is anyone learning to put away selfishness in order to sacrificially serve others?

The community of the church can be powerful because God is at work within us to mold us into maturity in Christ. We need each other to reach this maturity. We belong to each other. We are the body of Christ. Only in community can "we take our lead from Christ, who is the source of everything we do. He keeps us in step with each other. His very breath and blood flow through us, nourishing us so that we will grow up healthy in God, robust in love" (Ephesians 4:15-16).

Yes, community is essential to rediscovering the much older ways that will move us into the future. Community is discipleship living, and it's at the core of authentic Christianity in which

we intentionally work together for a common purpose, focus together on ministry in a common place, and share together what the Lord has given us in order to demonstrate the reality that Christ's kingdom has come.

Who wouldn't be attracted to that?

---

[1] Used with permission of Dr. Larry Crabb. Please find out more about this valued conference in the Resources section of this book, where you are encouraged to access Larry's New Way Ministries website, www.newwayministries.org.

[2] Robert E. Webber, *The Younger Evangelicals: Facing the Challenges of the New World* (Grand Rapids, Mich.: Baker, 2002), pp. 118-119.

[3] Lesslie Newbigin, *The Open Secret: An Introduction to a Theology of Mission*, rev. ed. (Grand Rapids, Mich.: Eerdmans, 1994), p. 150.

[4] Our thanks to Dave Wayman, one of the pastors at Woodmen Valley Chapel in Colorado Springs, Colorado, for his valued insights here.

[5] Used with permission from *An Unstoppable Force: Daring to Become the Church God Had in Mind* by Erwin Raphael McManus, published by Group Publishing, Inc., PO Box 481, Loveland, CO 80538 www.grouppublishing.com.

It's About Trusting God—
Not Technique

*The tools of our trade aren't for marketing or manipulation, but they are
for demolishing that entire massively corrupt culture. We use our powerful
God-tools for smashing warped philosophies, tearing down barriers erected
against the truth of God, fitting every loose thought and emotion and
impulse into the structure of life shaped by Christ. Our tools are
ready at hand for clearing the ground of every obstruction
and building lives of obedience into maturity.*

2 CORINTHIANS 10:4-6

Try this: For a month, save the invitations you receive to
attend yet another seminar promising a new "secret" for
growing your church or revitalizing your church life. In the past,
you probably have attended some of these workshops and have
tried to put some of the things you learned into practice.
However, as is the case with most expansive claims, you probably never discovered the "sure seminar secrets" that will radically
change your church in the ways it truly needs to change.

What's behind this never-ending quest to find the secrets of
success in ministry? We'd like to suggest that this pursuit has little to do with biblical principles and much to do with principles
that carried over to the modern world from the Enlightenment.

During the Age of Enlightenment in the eighteenth century,
people began to see the world as a great mechanical system.
With the right tweak or manipulation, the right part or technique,

you could change almost anything. That sounds just like most of those seminars we all get invited to.

Jacques Ellul talks about technique in his book *The Technological Society:* "In our technological society, *technique* is the *totality of methods rationally arrived at and having absolute efficiency* (for a given stage of development) in *every field* of human activity."[1] In the foreword to Ellul's book, Robert Merton explains, "Ours is a progressively technical civilization: By this Ellul means that the ever-expanding and irreversible rule of technique is extended to all domains of life."[2]

Relying on technique is an Enlightenment idea that has become ingrained in us. It's what we think with, not what we think about. It's one of the reasons we have so many how-to books for every idea and issue under the sun. This emphasis on technique, as Ellul explains, permeates all of today's society:

> The machine has made itself master of the heart and
> brain both of the average man and of the mob. What
> excites the crowd? Performance—whether performance
> in sports (the result of a certain sporting technique) or
> economic performance (as in the Soviet Union), in reality
> these are the same thing. Technique is the instrument of
> performance. What is important is to go higher and faster;
> the object of the performance means little. The act is suf-
> ficient unto itself. Modern man can think only in figures,
> and the higher the figures, the greater the satisfaction.[3]

Without even realizing it, many of us have adopted the Enlightenment model as a way of seeking success in ministry as well. Success is almost always defined as progress, and in our context, that often means church growth. This is why, in an often desperate search for answers, we are on a seemingly endless

search for the secret of church growth, among other "church secrets." If we're honest with ourselves, we really do believe we can grow our churches if we can just find the missing piece— the right technique (such as the right program or the most engaging worship style) that will bring success to all we do.

We probably don't need to tell you this, but church shopping is a reality. Like shopping for a car or a value meal, people look for the best deal when it comes to selecting a church. But before we blame the shoppers, let's remember that churches have become purveyors of religious goods and services.[4] We adopt an entrepreneurial and competitive attitude to recruit more numbers into the fold and to claim success in church business.

This consumerism within the church has led to what one friend in ministry refers to as serial monogamy.[5] People search for a church of their choice and settle in for a while. But they have no deep commitment. Eventually, these same consumers begin to dislike what's going on in their church, so they look around again and settle in somewhere else. They then repeat the pattern.

This isn't authentic Christianity. As pastors, we've become managers. We're taught to practice principles more related to business and marketing than to the practices of following Jesus. Then, we start to care more about bottom lines—of attendance, budgets, facilities, and programs—than we do about making disciples for Christ. This explains the comments of a Japanese businessman to a visiting Australian: "Whenever I meet a Buddhist leader, I meet a holy man. Whenever I meet a Christian leader, I meet a manager."[6] Ouch! But before you dismiss that thought, think about how true it is.

The church is the mission of God. The people we serve in our congregations are the community God calls out of the world in order to be sent into the world. If we want to meaningfully engage the world with the gospel of the kingdom, we need to disengage from the worldliness that captivates our hearts.

Because as the church we're "the dwelling in which God lives by his Spirit" (Ephesians 2:22, NIV), we're different in nature from the rest of the institutions that exist in the world. We possess a dual nature—both human and divine. God sends the church into the world to do battle against the powers of the Evil One and to proclaim reconciliation.[7]

Among other things, this means that as church leaders—as influencers within our communities—we must lead the way in presenting a clear alternative to the power structures of the world. We must learn afresh to walk by faith in the Lord. We need to change the object of our faith. It's easy for confidence in technique to become idolatry. We need to turn from our trust in technique to trust again in the Sovereign Lord of lords. We must repent again and actively believe the good news.

Right now, the Holy Spirit is inviting us to go on an amazing journey. As we leave the familiar shores of what we've known as Christendom and modernism to embark into the postmodern world, God is calling us to leave things that are familiar and comfortable. Maybe we don't even want to go on the trip. We may want things to be the way they used to be when Christianity was at the center of the culture. Perhaps we're still trying to rebuild what remains of the ruins of Christendom.

But the world won't go back to such a state. What about you?

We must, by faith in our triune God, move forward into uncharted territory. To do anything less would leave succeeding

generations without the message of the gospel of Jesus Christ. This new journey isn't merely an option if we're serious about our calling to be pastors and church leaders in the future.

Our present condition is like the wilderness experience of the children of Israel. God called them to leave their bondage in Egypt to go to the Promised Land. But the journey was filled with danger. Not only that, the children of Israel had become comfortable with their bondage. At least it was familiar and they knew what to expect. Doesn't this sound a lot like the church of today?

Striking out for the Promised Land required faith. Not all of them had the faith to make it. They saw the Lord perform great miracles for them. They even saw the presence of the Lord on Mount Sinai and the glory of the Lord shining on Moses' face. Yet they still yearned for the familiar. They missed the leeks and the garlic of Egypt. Some even mutinied against the Lord so they could go back.

It requires faith to go on this journey. It requires us to be leaders who have faith that the Lord is still with us through uncertain times. Don't forget God's promise: "Since God assured us, 'I'll never let you down, never walk off and leave you,' we can boldly quote, 'God is there ready to help; I'm fearless no matter what. Who or what can get to me?'" (Hebrews 13:5-6).

But you might wonder, "Where are we going?" At least the children of Israel had a clue about their destination. They knew they were headed to the Promised Land. But where is the church headed now?

Jesus' words give us a clue: "This is the rock on which I will put together my church, a church so expansive with energy that not even the gates of hell will be able to keep it out" (Matthew 16:18). If we're going to follow Jesus, if we're going to be a part of the church that he is building, then we are headed for the gates of hell.

Jesus is building his church to do battle with the forces of darkness in this present age. He isn't leading us to some comfy place. It's a battle zone, fraught with danger. We can expect casualties. But we can also expect something else: victory.

Jesus, the very same one who "disarmed the powers and authorities . . . triumphing over them by the cross" (Colossians 2:15, NIV), promises to be with us and to lead us into this battle. Because the church is empowered by his Spirit, we *will* overcome the gates of hell.

Of course, we have to be careful about our expectations for what that victory will look like or how it will be achieved. The ultimate victory is shrouded in mystery—to be revealed to us at the coming again of the Son of God. God wins victories by way of the Cross. If we minister in the name of Jesus, we'll minister by way of the Cross—denying ourselves daily and following Jesus.

Our hope can't be in the right technique. It must be in the power and presence of the Lord. His presence should give us great confidence to form, by the power of the Spirit, authentic Christian communities that proceed into the dangerous darkness with the light of the gospel.

What kind of faith will we need in this new setting for the church? Again, one of the prophets provides an answer:

> When the fig tree does not bud, and there are no grapes on the vines; when the olive trees do not produce, and the fields yield no crops; when the sheep disappear from the pen, and there are no cattle in the stalls, I will rejoice because of the Lord; I will be happy because of the God who delivers me. The sovereign Lord is my source of strength. He gives me the agility of a deer; he enables me to negotiate the rugged terrain. (Habakkuk 3:17-19, NET)

We can find hope in this passage for several reasons. First, it tells us that even in times of transition and danger, in times of hardship and privation, God is still at work. We need to retrain ourselves to recognize that God's blessing doesn't always come in terms of what we consider to be success. In fact, success in those terms may be utter failure. Even when we sense that nothing is happening, God may be working in our situation. God is still sovereign over history.

Second, this passage tells us where our real hope lies. Our hope isn't in the comfort of a prosperous situation but in the purposes of God. Authentic Christian communities and their leaders will suffer and sacrifice for the kingdom of God. Scripture tells us that "we must go through many hardships to enter the kingdom of God" (Acts 14:22, NIV). This is part of what it means to be a disciple of Jesus—to minister in Jesus' name. But despite the circumstances, we can look to the Lord to empower us and use us to fulfill his purposes. Our hope isn't found in better circumstances or even in the promise that the Lord will provide better circumstances. Our hope is in the Lord himself.[8]

Finally, part of the passage talks about the Lord giving his followers the agility of a deer—the skill of using their feet to get them where they need to be. For us, it means that the Lord will enable and empower us to go to the heights. These heights are rocky crags where only a deer will venture to go. In other words, these are the dangerous and difficult places that we'd probably not choose on our own. To these rugged places the Lord is leading us to do battle against the powers of this dark world. If we're going to fulfill the Lord's purposes for us, we need to reach these difficult places.

We heard a story about a Korean pastor who visited a large church in the southeastern United States. He noticed the lack of attendance for prayer at the Wednesday night service. On Thursday, the pastor of the church showed the visitor around his newly renovated facilities. He showed him the new educational wing, the overflow parking lot for vehicles at Sunday services, and the new sanctuary that would hold thousands of people. Toward the end of the tour, the American pastor turned to his counterpart and asked what he thought. The pastor from Korea simply responded, "It seems that you can do quite a bit without God."

Whether this story is true or apocryphal doesn't matter. What matters is the point it illustrates—a point that we need to take to heart. We can pursue success through technique to such an extent that we no longer hope in and trust God. Can anything we achieve through this method be even close to authentic Christianity?

Others will follow our leadership. But where are we leading our people? Are we teaching them to trust in technique, or are we training them toward faith in the Lord?

---

[1] Jacques Ellul, *The Technological Society* (New York: Random House, 1967), p. xxv.

[2] Robert Merton, foreword to *The Technological Society,* by Ellul, p. vi.

[3] Ellul, p. 302.

[4] George R. Hunsberger, "Features of the Missional Church: Some Directions and Pathways," *Reformed Review 52* (Autumn 1998): 5.

[5] We are indebted to Dr. Gary Westra for this insight.

[6] Quoted in Os Guinness, *Dining with the Devil* (Grand Rapids, Mich.: Baker, 1993), p. 49.

[7] We're indebted to Craig Van Gelder for these valuable insights from *The Essence of the Church: A Community Created by the Spirit* (Grand Rapids, Mich.: Baker, 2001), p. 31.

[8] Here we're paraphrasing a comment made by Larry Crabb in *Shattered Dreams: God's Unexpected Path to Joy* (Colorado Springs, Colo.: WaterBrook Press, 2001), p. 161.

It's About Following the Spirit—
Not Mere Strategizing

"Are your ears awake? Listen. Listen to the Wind Words,
the Spirit blowing through the churches."

REVELATION 3:6

One of the most rewarding days of my (Wes's) work with leadership teams is a day we call Future Think. I recently led one of these with a church that is new and small, but growing. I was especially sensitive to all that I was asking of the people of this dynamic fellowship. Because the church meets in a school, that Saturday morning we were meeting in a borrowed church hall. There was anticipation and excitement—in most people. A few were convinced that we were going against the Holy Spirit if we dared to hope, dream, or even plan forward.

What was happening within this young congregation was unnecessary chaos; thinking forward—beyond the excitement of starting something new—wasn't one of their bents. They were quite enamored with their "quick success," and now they were trying to do too much too soon. They'd made the error of strategizing very little and now felt they were sinking. And they were.

One thing that intrigued me about this congregation is that most of the members had started this new church because they were tired of the overstrategizing of their former churches.

Sadly, they had created a new church system (which really wasn't *that* new) out of reactions to their past. The future was hard for them to think about, as they were still nursing wounds from recent history.

No one spoke the following aloud, but they implied it through how they functioned: "We won't plan." Without realizing it, they were squeezing out the Holy Spirit from their midst. They were creating an organization where they, rather than God, would make things happen. They were forging a road where they wouldn't need to exercise their faith because they were going to make certain that the church tragedies of their past wouldn't take place in their future. While they still looked good on the outside, they were starting to smell bad on the inside. An insipid stagnancy was creeping in almost unnoticed.

Contrary to what this church believed, planning for the future of a church is not innately bad. It is, in fact, necessary to look toward the future as we seek to do God's will. However, as we get involved with our strategizing, we can lose sight of the dual nature of the church. Because the church is the dwelling place of the Holy Spirit, it's both human and divine. The sacred and creative delight of helping churches think forward is working with them to bring a wholeness and depth to their work that is not formulaic. Instead, it's based on what we learn God's design is for them. We must never lose sight of the fact that any congregation of any size or age of existence is God's church. It doesn't belong to anyone else.

Yet we still believe that we can grow the church. We often focus on the technical means of church growth, meanwhile losing sight of the fact that the church is a spiritual entity. We need to trust that the Spirit's unique gifts present in each member of a particular fellowship will determine what that church will be like in the future.

As the church keeps in step with the Spirit, catching the fresh winds of the Spirit, we'll be empowered to be the authentic Christian community that the Lord has called us to be in the world. It's not just a matter of bearing the fruit of the Spirit. It's also a matter of being led by the Spirit. The formation of our character, conformed to the image of Christ (catching the waves, as one surfing southern California pastor puts it), will enable us to minister effectively with the gospel of Jesus within our communities. We need to develop more sensitivity to what the Spirit is leading us to be and do.

You've probably heard this before. But sometimes we need to be reminded of the basics. We need to be reminded of God's original intent for his church. Before we receive what the Spirit is leading us to do, we must first concentrate on what the Spirit is leading us to be. So many of us focus on strategizing and the techniques we might use to build the church that we nearly forget the basics. The church will move into the future, not on the strength of our programming, but on the content of our character— a character formed by God's work within us.

We've become so consumer-driven that we've forgotten that our major work isn't programming or facility expansion; it's spiritual formation. That's what the Great Commission is all about— making disciples. We spend such an exorbitant amount of time and energy on strategizing that we seem to forget that the power of the church in the world is the work of God within us. He wants to change us and make us holy—disengaged from the world so that we might reengage with the world for the sake of the kingdom.[1]

So while we must "catch the waves" that the Spirit sends our way, we also need to remember that following the Spirit has to do with our own spiritual formation. Following the Spirit means walking with the Spirit and producing the fruit of the Spirit in our

lives. This fruit is what gives authenticity to whatever work we do.

Authenticity begins with our Christian character. But it doesn't end there. It also includes how we serve those who need to hear the gospel in a way that's meaningful to them. It has to do with enculturation. It involves an investment of our lives into the lives of others by listening and seeing, then speaking and doing in a way that is relevant.

Again, we often seem to be fixated on models. We look at what's working elsewhere, then try to implement those very same things within our ministries. Of course, other models of ministry can be helpful. But models usually aren't fully transferable. What works in other situations isn't always relevant in our own.

Thom Rainer puts it this way: "Most church strategies for intentionally reaching the unchurched in a particular community seem to be cookie-cutter approaches originating in areas that may have little in common with the church's community."[2] Maybe we need to start seeing that the success of some models simply shows that some churches are better than we are at catching the waves, thinking forward, creatively exercising their faith—better at being led by the Spirit.

Instead of looking carefully at the deep needs of our community and seeking direction from the Spirit to minister to those needs, we look to successful models and try to implement, piece by piece, what these other models have done. We use the same curriculum, sing the same music, borrow from their worship styles, and employ their technology. We do all of this without giving much attention to what the Spirit is saying to the church— especially to *our* particular church.

This leads to an important theological discussion: Is the Spirit saying anything to the church in our day? Is it possible to be led by the Spirit in the twenty-first century? For much of modern-day evangelicalism, there seems to be a lack of understanding about

the presence of the Holy Spirit within the church. Many of us don't see the Holy Spirit's practical relevance.

The church seems to be partitioned into two groupings— most likely you'll come up with even more. On the one hand is the noncharismatic (even anticharismatic) camp. They argue that at least certain gifts of the Spirit are no longer given in our day. They point to the completion of the canon of Scripture as the completion of God's revelation to us. They want to make sure that they distance themselves from any hint of what they often call "charismania." This group will tell you that they believe in the Holy Spirit—he's mentioned in the Creed; he's mentioned more than once in the Confession; he's a part of their Trinitarian formulas; their theological textbooks contain whole chapters dedicated to him. And they'll acknowledge that the Holy Spirit is still active in the hearts of people who are being saved.

If you fall into this camp, you need to answer a question. Apart from the pages of your doctrinal discourses, what *practical* relevance does the Holy Spirit have in your day-to-day operations within the church?

On the other hand is the charismatic camp (which has many variations). This group is happy to talk about the Holy Spirit as a present reality. They recognize the presence of the Holy Spirit in the gifting that he gives to the church. But many in this camp also seem to think that the Holy Spirit exists to provide us with some weird form of entertainment. They look for spectacular signs.

But when you cut through all the dazzling displays, the question still remains for those of you who endorse this viewpoint: What *practical* relevance does the Holy Spirit have in the day-to-day operations of your church? Are you really being led by the Spirit?

Many of us seem to operate as if the Holy Spirit isn't even

present within us. We act as if we have to make it on our own. So we break out the charts and do our strategizing. We get busy doing the work of God as if the Spirit has gone on sabbatical. We no longer listen for the leading of the Holy Spirit because we no longer believe that he has any practical relevance. We resort to technique. We resort to strategizing. We relegate the Holy Spirit to a point of doctrine. Even prayer becomes a form of technique to get what we want from God.

In the New Testament, especially the book of Acts, the Holy Spirit was active in the life of the church. The Holy Spirit had a practical relevance in its leading and direction. The Holy Spirit led Phillip to the Ethiopian eunuch. The Spirit set aside Paul and Barnabas for missionary work throughout the empire. The Holy Spirit prevented Paul from preaching in Asia, leading him into Macedonia instead. The Jerusalem Council was able to make a decision on the place of Gentile believers in the church and report their decision by saying, "It seemed good to the Holy Spirit and to us not to burden you with anything beyond the following requirements" (Acts 15:28, NIV).

If the Bible is truly our only infallible rule of faith and practice, how can we wonder if the presence of the Holy Spirit in the church has evaporated? As Christ-followers, we are not on our own. God is still present with us. Knowing this is true, how then do we follow the leading of the Spirit? Here are a few suggestions.[3]

First, let's trust that the Holy Spirit is still present and active in the church and in our lives today. Let's open our hearts to the reality of the Holy Spirit and seek his direction.

Second, let's allow the Word of God to guide us in all of our deliberations. The Holy Spirit will only work in ways consistent with God's Word. Let's affirm that any direction other than where the Bible leads us will be dangerous and defective.

Third, let's remember that the Holy Spirit is given corporately

to the church. Therefore, we must listen to one another. We need to stop trying to ram our own agendas through in our churches. Instead, we must learn to investigate matters with each other, talk to one another, and listen to one another. Let's set aside the time to pray together. We must learn to seek consensus of direction, believing that the Holy Spirit is leading and guiding us.

Fourth, let's be sensitive to God's providence. In his sovereignty, God places our churches in unique situations. Specific needs must be addressed in each place we serve. From church to church, these needs may be similar, but each congregation also has its own distinct shortcomings. Let's study our communities as well to find the primary needs our churches might address outside our walls. Let's look for the mix of gifts the Spirit has given our churches to see if we are capable of addressing those needs. If so, let's make plans to address them as the Lord provides.

Fifth, let's learn to wait on the Lord's provision. Not all the needs that exist in our communities have to be addressed right now. Some will have to wait for financial support, human resources, or a God-given burden to meet them. Remember that the Holy Spirit prevented the apostle Paul from preaching the gospel in Asia (see Acts 16:6). Surely people there needed to hear the gospel, but God had other plans.

We can still do our strategizing. But let it never be mere strategizing. Instead, let all of our planning be done under the direction of the Word and the Spirit. If we're to return to the much older ways, then we must learn to be more God-dependent and Spirit-directed. Imagine what that would be like.

---

[1] Darrell L. Guder, *Missional Church: A Vision for the Sending of the Church in North America* (Grand Rapids, Mich.: Eerdmans, 1998), p. 117.

² Thom S. Rainer, *Surprising Insights from the Unchurched and Proven Ways to Reach Them* (Grand Rapids, Mich.: Zondervan, 2001), p. 37.

³ We want to make it clear that we're not suggesting that we are experts on this subject. This may be a case of the blind leading the blind. But let's go forward, in his Spirit, together.

It's About Servanthood— Not Power

*Here's my concern: that you care for God's flock with all the diligence of a
shepherd. Not because you have to, but because you want to please God.
Not calculating what you can get out of it, but acting spontaneously.
Not bossily telling others what to do, but tenderly showing them the way.*

1 PETER 5:2-3

It was intriguing to sit with a group of associate pastors
recently. The purpose of the gathering was not to dump on
or tear apart current or past church ministry experiences but to
come together to consider what the next steps for these pastors
might look like if they sensed God calling them to become a lead
pastor (or senior pastor) in a church. These were good men and
women—vibrant, optimistic, faithful people who longed for God
to use them within his kingdom in the future.

At one point in the discussion, one person asked the other
members of the group how they would do church differently
from what they had experienced. Nearly all said they didn't want
to emulate the power and control they saw in too many senior
pastors. They voiced hope that they wouldn't succumb to the
power trips they'd been subjected to.

The conversation could have deteriorated there. But it didn't.
These younger leaders kept coming back to their desire to be
the kind of future shepherds that served in ways they hadn't

witnessed other pastors serving when they started in ministry. The conversation ended with hope—if hope comes from following Jesus' statement that he came to serve, not to be served (see Matthew 20:28).

We know few pastors who would disagree with that verse. They know it forward and backward. Yet not enough take time to live it in the rush of doing church business.

Get together with any group of pastors for a while and you'll hear quite a bit of talk about power. Many pastors want to gain power in their churches. Or they want to maintain power. Or they fear they're losing power.

You'll also hear a lot of talk about power struggles within the church. These power plays usually take place when a faction in the church gains enough strength to bully the rest of the church into doing things their way. Often, these battles stem from the people who control finances or whose family has been at the church the longest.

Money has become a great source of power within the church. People decide that if they don't get things their way, they'll withhold their giving. Maybe if they withhold their money long enough, they think, they can get the pastor to resign. Then they'll have a shot at getting *their* person in place—someone who will see things their way.

But money isn't the only source of power. So are raw numbers. The majority either votes on the budget or votes for the board members who set the budget. People who will vote "your way" are a source of power.

Interestingly, in the New Testament we don't see votes being taken within the church. Somehow the leaders of the early church were able to get God's work done without elections or Robert's Rules of Order. As church leaders served from a servant's heart, there was little concern about their "power."

This concern for power today seems especially true of new pastors. When pastors haven't been around long enough to build trust, they focus instead on building a power base for maintaining their control over the church. They feel the need to prove themselves by being successful with their agenda.

This type of power struggle is often a delicate interplay between the pastor, various boards, and the "power brokers" of the church, both formal and informal. In fact, students graduating from seminary and pastors changing churches should check into who the informal leaders are in a prospective church, for they often wield more influence in a church body than the appointed and anointed leaders. These informal leaders are well acquainted with the weapons of money and numbers. As they broker for power, they can create reasons to demand change in pastoral leadership.

Sadly, such happenings are all too familiar. Perhaps you've not just heard the horror stories. Maybe you've lived through them as well.

Not only do too many pastors concern themselves with power struggles within the congregation, but some also seek to gain power through other means. Some use the power of prestige. Others bank on the power of success. Still others wield the power of what we might call "being on the cutting edge."

Other pastors move quickly from church to church. A friend in the business world recently told us that it's now a liability for someone in business to remain in one place of employment for a long time. When long-term employees look for another job, they're viewed as having no drive or motivation. They should have been moving around from job to job and constantly climbing the

ladder of success instead of being faithfully employed in one place.[1] They either lack spunk or they're ignorant of the present realities of the business world. They're probably not motivated by the bottom line. In any case, they're a liability.

Has this same attitude infiltrated the church? Too many senior pastors think only of the business or the bottom line of church. The externals of image, couched in exciting rhetoric, become what count. People in the pew buy this for a while and then move on.

Senior and associate pastor positions in many churches, especially smaller ones, are often seen only as stepping-stones to better places of service. Sadly, youth workers are notorious for staying in a position for only fifteen to eighteen months. Though varying factors contribute to this, many become involved in a cycle of "I'll move on if I don't like it here" or "It will look good on my résumé as I move on to better places."

Thankfully, many involved men and women are engaged in pastoral ministry for the long haul—in vital places of service that are small and unknown. God bless them!

We hope that you're a pastor who really believes you're engaged in God's work in the world and that you truly desire to accomplish the Lord's will in and through the ministry that he's placed in your care—no matter the size of your congregation. Small shouldn't be seen as a weakness, just as large shouldn't be seen as a burden or something to envy.

The Incarnation—the life and death of Jesus—demonstrates that God's purposes are accomplished through weakness, not through the power structures of the world. Christ opposed and conquered the powers of the world through weakness: "And having disarmed the powers and authorities, he made a public spectacle of

them, triumphing over them by the cross" (Colossians 2:15, NIV).

The early church demonstrated this same weakness. We remember from church history that members of the church were outcast, outlawed, persecuted, and exiled. Through its weakness, the church sowed the seeds of the gospel and produced fruit. Despite its weakness, the work of God was accomplished.

Both the incarnation of our Lord Jesus and the witness of the early church demonstrate that the church is called to oppose the power structures of the world through weakness. Greatness in the kingdom requires the weakness of servanthood. Let's help each other remember that.

As pastors, do we take a stand against the power structures of the world? Or have we instead adopted them as our way of doing things? If we're honest with ourselves, we'll have to recognize that in many instances we've used these power structures to manipulate people into the kingdom. In terms of our witness before the world, we've refused to be weak or to be fools for Jesus. We've become a most worldly church.

Sadly, we've learned to rely on the power of celebrity in the church. We turn to the world of sports or entertainment to get our latest witnesses for Jesus. Such people can provide the "hook" we need to draw a large crowd. Of course, it's great when anyone uses who they are to proclaim faith in Jesus. But no longer does the power of a transformed life make our witness credible. No, now we turn to more popular things like Super Bowl rings, boxing belts, and Grammy or Dove awards. We wield this power of celebrity in such a way that we infer that Jesus will make people winners or champions or stars. The

message seems to be "Win with Jesus" or "Be somebody with Jesus" instead of "Deny yourself, pick up a cross, and follow Jesus."

But that's not all. Even Christian speakers, musicians, authors, and evangelists reach celebrity status now. They have their own following, their own entourage. Instead of the humbling words of John the Baptist to guide us (see John 3:30), we now say in effect, *"I* must increase so that he may increase." Somehow, we believe that we can use the power of celebrity as a way to proclaim a gospel that came in weakness and foolishness. How do we rationalize the difference?

We've learned to rely on the power of consumerism as well. Our concern to be seeker-driven or seeker-sensitive has a profound effect on our worship as a community of God's people. We admit that people are shopping when they attend our services, and we mold our services to that reality in several ways.

We replace worship with entertainment. We substitute the preaching of God's Word with self-help lessons that offer formulas for "how to . . . in a few easy steps." We rely on the power of materialism. We become concerned about offering a quality product. We want our churches to be spacious, comfortable, and equipped with the latest in modern technology. We design our services to be impressive. Our music features hot licks and great sound. Like a chef in a gourmet restaurant, we're concerned about presentation. Image reigns.

Our critique of these practices is not an excuse to offer shoddiness in the presentation of the gospel. That's not the point. We should enjoy the good sound and the hot licks. We must pay attention to details. We do need to encourage and affirm workers, bestowing honor on the unsung heroes of our congregations and communities.

Yet while recognizing all of this, we need to work at living

with the truth that the gospel isn't about the good life. It's not about getting more out of life. We must stop relying on materialism as a means to promote a gospel that requires self-denial— a gospel that calls us to follow a homeless carpenter from such a suspicious place as Nazareth.

In addition, we've learned to rely on the power of professionalism. The care of souls, the equipping of the saints for ministry, and the ministry of the Word and prayer have often been replaced in the evangelical church by the running of church business by modern managers. If we just rely on the proper techniques, we believe that *we* can grow the church to a place of prominence and power within our society.

Finally, we've learned to rely on the power of numbers. We claim that numbers are significant. Not only do we try to impress each other with the number of people who attend our services, but we also use our numbers to intimidate our way in public policy matters—to overturn court decisions or to forge our platform on a political agenda.

It's not that we don't have a vote—we do. And it's not that our vote doesn't matter—it does. But this intimidation factor and reliance on the power of numbers demonstrates the fact that we've adopted the power structures of the world. Numbers tell us some things. But do they tell us the most important, life-transforming things?

The church learned to trust in the power structures of the world during the time of the early formation of Christendom. During those centuries, it learned to wield political and worldly power to "Christianize" society. Church leaders from the Christendom era would compel the state to call for councils to set straight matters

of doctrine, punish heretics, call for armies to take back the Holy Land, and make new Christians. During Christendom, we learned to operate by the power of coercion rather than to invite people to conversion.

Much of this has filtered down to our day. We still think we can use the power structures of the world to make people Christians. The powers we now employ have the appearance of being kinder and gentler, but they're still worldly powers. People still read us correctly when they sense that we're trying to manipulate them.[2]

I (Glenn) learned about people's fear of being manipulated when I offered that our church would help with some events held in our town. I can still remember the first meeting I had with the recreation committee that oversees these events. They were very wary of our participation. It was a new thing for a church to offer to help, and they figured that we had a hidden agenda in our involvement.

They made it clear that we were not to pass out any "propaganda"—as they called it—at these functions. I'm pretty sure they thought that condition would be the end of our involvement with them. But we persevered in just wanting to be servants to our community. As a result, we not only have an improved relationship with the recreation committee but a better reputation with the people of our local community as well. They're learning to trust us.

Throughout Christendom, we've been relying on the world's power structures, but Jesus shows us a better way. To be great in his kingdom means that as the community of God's people, we need to learn to be servants. We need to work at embracing

opportunities, especially when our churches are pushed to the margins of the culture. It's an exciting new approach to ministry in our world. This is a hard thought, but it will also bring us freedom to serve well if we're willing to be weak and to be fools— to be like Jesus, who "did not come to be served, but to serve, and to give his life as a ransom for many" (Matthew 20:28, NIV).

Becoming servants to our world requires a very intentional reorientation of our thinking. Too often, we focus on being grand or spectacular, as if the greatness of an event or a program will captivate the attention of the people we're seeking to minister to. While we seek after excellence and entertainment as a way to reach the world, we haven't yet learned that we can't outdo the world's whistles, bells, and thrills.

The world can entertain more successfully than we can. But we have something far better, far richer, and far deeper to offer. We can offer life. And life is found nowhere else but in the Son of Man who came to serve.

Learning to be servants means learning to be patient. It means serving as if no one is noticing. People will notice—eventually. But it will take repeated efforts and a consistent life of service for people to get it. Let's plan to serve for the long term and not demand great results right away.

Being servants calls us again and again to trust in God. It takes faith to go to dangerous places in the name of Jesus. It takes trust in the Lord to do things over and over without immediate results. It takes a confidence in the One we're living a life of service for—confidence that his reward is really enough.

Servanthood calls us to our knees to pray that the Lord will work in our simple acts of kindness or generosity. It calls us to believe that God can use our simple actions to accomplish his great works.

In Exodus 3, we're told of the calling of Moses to deliver the

people of God from bondage in Egypt. Moses, you remember, had a royal upbringing as the son of Pharaoh's daughter in the courts of Egypt. By the time we get to Exodus 3, those days of Moses' life are long behind him. At this point, he's a shepherd. In fact, he's been a shepherd for quite a long time. And now God is calling him back to deliver the people of Israel from their slavery.

Like most of us, Moses wondered if he was fit for this work. He thought of many reasons why he shouldn't return. He offered a lot of excuses.

"What is that in your hand?" God asked Moses. It was only a staff—little more than a long stick. God told Moses to take his stick and go back to Egypt. It wasn't much to go on. Or was it?

Moses learned that by the power of God, his stick could turn into a snake. Later, he would take his staff and smack it into the Nile River, turning the water to blood. Some time after that, Moses would raise that stick over the Red Sea and view with his own eyes the great deliverance of the people of Israel from their Egyptian captors. On another occasion, he would keep that shepherd's staff raised above his head and watch the armies of Israel defeat their enemies in battle.

God didn't use Moses' royal education to accomplish his great purposes. God chose to use a shepherd with a stick. Our faith is in a God who can use sticks to bring about deliverance for his people.

Acts of service to others will help us put the "go" back in the Great Commission. Often our strategy hasn't been one of "go" but one of "come." We call the world to come to our churches— "come and fit in here." But that's only effective within a Christendom context, because these days people have many

other places to go on Sunday mornings or Wednesday nights. As we move into the future, we and our congregations need to learn to go again. What an adventure! We're called to go and be servants to the glory of God.

A final word for those of you in pastoral ministry. Servanthood can be a defining mark of your ministry. Because you lead by example, you can be a servant to people both inside and outside your church. Maybe you're among the many pastors who don't need to hear these words. Perhaps you serve every day with a servant's heart. If so, thank you for your example of selflessness. Your simple acts of kindness and graciousness haven't gone unnoticed. Your life models servanthood to your congregation and to your community.

But if you're one of those pastors who believes that some tasks are beneath you—below the dignity of your office—remember the Head of the church. He left the glory of heaven to become a servant. He took on human flesh in order to die a cruel death on the cross. To this day, he sits enthroned in heaven with the scars he received on this earth. No high-ranking pastor is greater than this Master of servanthood.

Entitlement isn't the way of the Cross. Servanthood is. Let's be about doing his business in his way, all for his great honor and glory.

---

[1] We encourage you to read Bill Thrall, Bruce McNicol, and Ken McElrath, *The Ascent of a Leader: How Ordinary Relationships Develop Extraordinary Character and Influence* (San Francisco: Jossey-Bass, 1999). This is an exceptional book on the character of leadership and what happens when we climb the right ladder.

[2] An important book on the future of evangelism in the church is Brian McLaren, *More Ready Than You Realize: Evangelism As Dance in the Postmodern Matrix* (Grand Rapids, Mich.: Zondervan, 2002).

It's About Fruit—
Not Achievement

*"Listen carefully: Unless a grain of wheat is buried in the ground, dead to
the world, it is never any more than a grain of wheat. But if it is buried,
it sprouts and reproduces itself many times over."*

JOHN 12:24

Sometimes it's a surprise to people outside of church work
to find out just how busy "doing the ministry" is.
Sometimes it seems like it's 29 hours a day, 8 days a week, 39
days a month, and 392 days a year!

We don't know about you, but the two commodities that
often seem to be lacking in our lives are time and money. Don't
get us wrong. As part of two ministry couples, we're blessed in
many ways. But sometimes we just stop and look at our
spouses—and laugh at where we find ourselves! Even with
money tight sometimes, we're blessed way beyond what others
experience. And yet that "busy-demon" keeps creeping up on us.
Giving time and attention to the right priorities—both personally
and in ministry—seems to be one of the most persistent battles
we face.

If you have conquered this, please write or call *soon!*

Let's talk about busyness and what's important—and not
important—to our ministry. Why do we sometimes yield to the
persistent pressures of ministry and get too busy? If we're honest

with ourselves, we get overly busy when we try to live up to other people's expectations. People expect to be visited, especially if they're ill or hospitalized. People have expectations about administration and communication within the church. In some smaller churches, people may even expect us to be involved in building maintenance. Most of us have found that trying to live up to other people's expectations traps us in a maze of busyness. We live with a fear that if we don't meet the expectations of our congregations, we may be out of a job.

Other expectations come from being part of a church association or denomination; this commitment might include being involved in some kind of committee or project. It can be hard to turn down these appeals because we're constantly trying to maintain or improve our reputations within our denominations. Within the culture of Western Christianity, we need to build bridges and keep our options open to further our careers. This sounds awful. And it is. But we know it's truer than we like to admit. It's a tough world out there—even in the "church world."

Our colaborers in kingdom causes—fellow pastors in our local communities—also have expectations of us. They may want us to be involved in some form of mission project in our community. These projects often require organization, planning, and energy.

Even pastors of smaller churches can become involved in a whole host of time-consuming, energy-sapping activities. Taking mission trips, serving on boards, and assisting with citywide events are just a few examples. Sometimes this leads to hobnobbing with the "big boys"—nationally known speakers, evangelists, or politicians—as they attend seminars devoted to some aspect of ministry.

As we strive to meet these expectations we learn that we can stay pretty busy and appear to be fairly important.

Sometimes our quest for busyness grows out of the disappointment of pastoring smaller churches. After years of training and tasting "success" at larger churches, it can be a letdown to wind up as the pastor of a smaller church.

Remember, growth and size aren't bad. We're not trying to promote one over another. But we always need to be concerned first with inner growth and transformation—no matter what size church we pastor. Our main priority when we're "doing church" needs to be what's happening in the hearts and lives and relationships of our people and the impact we're having on our community. Anything less isn't doing church God's way.

Consider Paul's exuberant depth of joy and concern for the folks in the churches in Colossae and Ephesus. Do your best to read slowly here. Settle into your soul for a bit. Ponder well the intent of the words. If necessary, grab your own well-worn and familiar Bible and read these words again. But read them as our triune God's words to you—just you—where you are in location and where you are in your heart:

I greet the Christians and stalwart followers of Christ who live in Colossae. . . .

I want you to know how glad I am that it's me sitting here in this jail and not you. There's a lot of suffering to be entered into in this world—the kind of suffering Christ takes on. I welcome the chance to take my share in the church's part of that suffering. When I became a servant in this church, I experienced this suffering as a sheer gift, God's way of helping me serve you, laying out the whole truth.

This mystery has been kept in the dark for a long time, but now it's out in the open. God wanted everyone, not just Jews, to know this rich and glorious secret

inside and out, regardless of their background, regardless of their religious standing. The mystery in a nutshell is just this: Christ is in you, therefore you can look forward to sharing in God's glory. It's that simple. That is the substance of our Message. We preach *Christ,* warning people not to add to the Message. We teach in a spirit of profound common sense so that we can bring each person to maturity. To be mature is to be basic. Christ! No more, no less. That's what I'm working so hard at day after day, year after year, doing my best with the energy God so generously gives me.

I want you to realize that I continue to work as hard as I know how for you, and also for the Christians over at Laodicea. Not many of you have met me face-to-face, but that doesn't make any difference. Know that I'm on your side, right alongside you. You're not in this alone.

I want you woven into a tapestry of love, in touch with everything there is to know of God. Then you will have minds confident and at rest, focused on Christ, God's great mystery. All the richest treasures of wisdom and knowledge are embedded in that mystery and nowhere else. And we've been shown the mystery! I'm telling you this because I don't want anyone leading you off on some wild-goose chase, after other so-called mysteries, or "the Secret."

I'm a long way off, true, and you may never lay eyes on me, but believe me, I'm on your side, right beside you. I am delighted to hear of the careful and orderly ways you conduct your affairs, and impressed with the solid substance of your faith in Christ. . . .

It's in Christ that we find out who we are and what

we are living for. Long before we first heard of Christ and got our hopes up, he had his eye on us, had designs on us for glorious living, part of the overall purpose he is working out in everything and everyone.

It's in Christ that you, once you heard the truth and believed it (this Message of your salvation), found yourselves home free—signed, sealed, and delivered by the Holy Spirit. This signet from God is the first installment on what's coming, a reminder that we'll get everything God has planned for us, a praising and glorious life.

That's why, when I heard of the solid trust you have in the Master Jesus and your outpouring of love to all the Christians, I couldn't stop thanking God for you—every time I prayed, I'd think of you and give thanks. But I do more than thank. I ask—ask the God our Master, Jesus Christ, the God of glory—to make you intelligent and discerning in knowing him personally, your eyes focused and clear, so that you can see exactly what it is he is calling you to do, grasp the immensity of this glorious way of life he has for Christians, oh, the utter extravagance of his work in us who trust him—endless energy, boundless strength!

All this energy issues from Christ: God raised him from death and set him on a throne in deep heaven, in charge of running the universe, everything from galaxies to governments, no name and no power exempt from his rule. And not just for the time being, but *forever*. He is in charge of it all, has the final word on everything. At the center of all this, Christ rules the church. The church, you see, is not peripheral to the world; the world is peripheral to the church. The church is Christ's body, in which he speaks and acts, by

which he fills everything with his presence. (Colossians 1:2,24–2:5, Ephesians 1:11-23)

Whoa! Amazing words. Read them again!

What would you do if Paul wrote those words directly to you in your situation? Busyness causes us to forget our core purposes as pastors and leaders within his church.

This is a trick of the enemy of our souls—that scoundrel who's always trying to stop us from living out our calling. We might think God has something more in mind for us if we just stay busy for him. For example, you may think to yourself, *I might only be pastor of a small church, but I can also be president of the local Jaycees, serve as a chaplain for the police department, and be active on a denominational committee.* But this kind of thinking stems from our own egos.

We all want to believe that what we're doing is important—that it matters in some transcendent way. We all want to make our lives count for something. When we are honest with ourselves, our busyness has to do with this very thing. Maybe it seems nothing substantial is happening in our church. But a church of any size isn't going to quench our thirst for significance.

It's interesting that Paul wrote some of his most meaningful words when he had time to think, ponder, pray, and write from his heart—in jail. We don't usually think of people doing time in jail as having much to offer. But Scripture tells us a different story.

We consistently need to come to grips with the fact that our own models of success and the plans of God don't always coincide. His plans don't always square with our expectations for success; his ways aren't our ways. Don't gloss over that last sentence. His ways, your ways, my ways—they're not the same.

God doesn't see size or numbers as significant. Society looks

on the outward appearance—the nickels, numbers, and noise. The Lord looks on the heart. We find ourselves searching for something significant simply because we forget or fail to understand that God has already given us something significant in our smaller, struggling churches.

Why do so many of us believe that pastoring a smaller church might not matter as much? Why do we get so busy being involved in a number of other things as if they do matter?

Making disciples of a small group of people is powerfully important. It's exactly the kind of work that Jesus did. He had the courage and vision to think small, and so should we. Why do we think that building big churches is, in and of itself, obedience to the Great Commission, when the imperative of that commandment is to "make disciples"? It's not based on size. (Maybe we need to lose the "Great" and rename it simply "the Commission.") Success in the eyes of men—even other men and women in the ministry—isn't necessarily success in the eyes of God.

Busyness keeps us from the face of God. It keeps us from allowing him to probe into our hearts and to ask his searing questions regarding our ministries and lives. We easily use busyness both to salve our consciences and to hide ourselves from God's higher assessment. Then we run out of gas because we've removed our hearts from their eternal power source.

Remember the story of Martha and Mary (see Luke 10:38-42)? Martha, like so many of us, was busy. Mary sat at her Master's feet. At the feet of Jesus, we see someone who is teachable, someone who has a heart to be a disciple, and someone who understands that what needs to be produced in her life can only come from dependence on God.

We say we want to be with Jesus, but our busyness disproves that voiced longing. Sitting at the feet of Jesus demonstrates a

willingness to allow him to rule and reign in our lives. At the feet of Jesus, we realize that our value is found in our identity with him.

If we desire to return to the much older ways, then we must come face-to-face with the fact that authentic ministry is about fruit, not achievement. The difference between fruit and achievement is found in the production models they result from. The production of fruit comes out of an organic model. Achievement comes out of a mechanical model. It's the difference between an orchard and a factory. Both are modes of production, but they're quite different.

In the summer of 2001, some of our best friends traveled with my wife and me (Wes) to the place where I was raised in Oregon. Though much had changed over the decades, I was pleasantly surprised to find two pear trees laden down with exceptional fruit in one of our old pastures. I even have a photo to prove this story.

I remember the day from my childhood when my parents got into a heated disagreement because my father allowed a horticulture professor from Oregon State University to "really trim back" those two pear trees. It looked like he had killed them. His purpose? To graft some new varieties of pears onto healthy stock.

In the first couple of years after that event in the early fifties, it looked like the professor had done a horrible deed. But he apparently knew what he was doing after all. Now, nearly fifty years later, the trees were bearing so much exceptional fruit that the limbs needed to be propped up. I could still see several varieties of pears coming from the same two trunks. I quietly thought, *Someday, this will "preach" somewhere.*

I don't like being pruned. When I've been severely pruned, I wonder if growth of any kind will ever happen again. But we have a "heavenly professor" who knows what he's doing when he places us in our particular pastures for his purposes and prunes us to bear his fruit.

The Bible consistently uses the organic model as a way to describe our life in relationship with God. Jesus uses it in his parables of the kingdom. Paul calls upon us to bear the fruit of the Spirit by living in a relationship with the Holy Spirit. Jesus tells us, "I am the Vine, you are the branches. When you're joined with me and I with you, the relation intimate and organic, the harvest is sure to be abundant. Separated, you can't produce a thing" (John 15:5).

The question that we need to be asking ourselves is this: In all our busyness—our chasing after achievement or significance—are we producing any fruit? Fruit, after all, is what Jesus expects from us. Fruitfulness, not achievement, needs to be our goal.

It might be helpful to compare the two different models of production. Let's look first at the biblical organic model.

The organic model shows us that fruit is produced naturally. It's a natural byproduct of a healthy organism. A plant yields fruit when all the organic systems are healthy and the plant is properly nourished and even properly pruned from time to time.

If you asked an apple farmer about the care of his apple orchard, he'd tell you that he has plenty of things to do. Sometimes he must prune off old, dead branches that are unproductive. And he must sometimes prune shoots that are very much alive but that will sap the tree of its strength and productivity if they keep growing. This will allow the strong, growing branches of the tree to be as productive as they were designed to be.

Checking the condition of the soil is also critical. The farmer needs to make certain that the soil has the proper organic blends

(back home in Oregon, we called these "organic blends" plain old cow manure) that will allow the trees to perform at their peak. Then he may need to use pesticides to keep the trees from being eaten by predator insects. He must set up forms of protection from birds that might destroy the crop. And he may need to irrigate to keep the trees alive.

But when the trees are in the right relationship with the soil, water, and sun and they receive the protection and nourishment they need, they produce fruit naturally—all by themselves. With some faith, diligence, and perseverance, the farmer enjoys a season of the fruits of his labors before the cycle of life begins again. This is how God designed it, not just for trees, but for us as well.

This is the picture that Jesus gives us of our relationship with him. When we allow the Lord to prune what is dead and cut off the branches that will sap our spiritual energy, when we live in a healthy relationship with the Lord, and when we ask for protection from predators, we naturally produce fruit. This model is not only true for us as individuals; it's true for our families, our friends, and our colaborers in kingdom causes. It can also be true in our lives, relationships, and ministries.

Being pruned isn't a picnic. But enjoying fruit is. Will you trust the process? Are you willing to trust the Lord to have his way in and through you?

The mechanical model is different, and many of us prefer it because we think we can control the process. In this model, having the right machinery and the right people in place is all-important. In fact, in this environment we tend to reduce people to being cogs in the machinery of production. This model rarely works to help people develop lasting relationships.

Be honest with yourself. Do you view your people this way? Do you have to be hands-on? Is it hard to trust others in your life?

In the mechanical model, time becomes important. We spend a great deal of energy on time management and efficiency. While a farmer patiently waits for his fruit to grow, the mechanical model drives the factory owner to produce, so he drives his workers and machinery to produce as well. It all needs to be cost and time efficient.

The mechanical model assigns a value to production. If a factory worker is inefficient, we'll replace him. If a tech company worker is productive, we may reward her. If a new machine or computer program can perform better, we'll purchase it to take the place of the old one. However, these people and things have no intrinsic value. We value only the production itself.

Which of these two models best describes the way you and your church operate? Do you see your people as having intrinsic value—as being potential fruit bearers? Or are they merely cogs for your programs and platforms? Are you patient with your people, both paid and unpaid, waiting for God to do his work in them in his good time? Or are you impatient, wishing you could replace them with people who'll get more done or driving them to produce unnaturally according to your time frame?

I (Wes) was sickened to hear recently of a pastor who told his staff, "You do your best to make this church look good and to make me look good to the church. If I look good, then you'll look good. And then God will look good, too. If you can't do that, maybe you don't belong here."

We all need to read—annually, if possible—Gordon MacDonald's classic book *Ordering Your Private World*. MacDonald speaks clearly to the issue of drivenness that many of us live with (without stopping and trying to find out why). We find it so easy to defend our schedules, yet our defense is truly puny, even in the midst of very trying issues in people's lives that daily demand our time.

As pastors, we're not the only ones on the planet who lead hectic lives. Circumstances will always demand our time. But if we can come to grips with our own busyness, we can model for our people how to live life. What will we show them tomorrow, next month, and next year?

The biblical model of the church is organic. The Lord is seeking fruitfulness from our lives. Jesus says that a fruitful life will occur naturally as we live in a healthy relationship with him. Therefore our focus shouldn't be "What am I accomplishing?" Instead, it must be "Am I (and my flock) living in a healthy relationship with the Lord?" How will you know? You and your fellow disciples of Jesus will bear fruit, individually and corporately. You'll see healthy and creative evidence of the fruit of the Spirit produced in your own life and in the lives of the people you minister to.

We must take the lead in demonstrating our dependence on the Lord. Like Mary, we need to stop being consumed with our busyness and learn to sit at the feet of Jesus. We need to stop yielding to the expectations of those around us. We need to stop leaning into the unrealistic expectations we place on ourselves. We need to learn to be patient, waiting on the Lord to produce in us the harvest that he promises us—even if the rewards don't show up until heaven.

This doesn't mean that we'll sit around, twiddle our fingers, scratch our toes, and do nothing. It means that our focus will change. We'll focus on the things that make the environments in our churches and communities capable of bearing fruit.

We'll nurture our people in the rich soil of the Word of God. We'll train them to be God-dependent. We'll come to grips personally with the ways of the new covenant and help our flock understand how to live in freedom rather than bondage. We'll teach them by word and example to cut away things from their

lives that sap them of spiritual strength. They'll know more of what to do and be because they'll watch us respond to God's pruning that adds grace to our lives as he intends.

Instead of looking at the failures of our people, we'll instead see their need for further nourishment so they can produce fruit. Instead of driving them to become what we expect of them, we'll patiently wait for the Lord to do his work in their hearts as we continue to minister to them with the nutrients they need. It takes time to produce a crop.

Why not get started right now? Repent of your mechanical model. Stop treating your people like workers in a consumer-driven religion factory. Start by seeking God in your life and in your ministry. Ask him for the fresh wind of his Spirit. Learn to rely on the Lord rather than your own means of production. Adjust your schedule to spend time nurturing faith in your people rather than seeking to get more out of them.

If you do this, in time you can reach out to those who don't yet know the Lord with a peace of heart that trusts God to work in their lives and draw them to himself. You can stop being a frantic salesclerk for your religious "products" and instead live in a way that demonstrates your trust in God to bring in the harvest.

Then, with the angels, you can hold a thanksgiving party for what God has done. We'd love to celebrate this with you anytime. And our God waits to be invited to your party.

It's About Listening—
Not Just Preaching

Post this at all the intersections, dear friends: Lead with your ears,
follow up with your tongue, and let anger straggle along in the rear. . . .
Don't fool yourself into thinking that you are a listener when you are any-
thing but, letting the Word go in one ear and out the other. Act on what you
hear! Those who hear and don't act are like those who glance in the mirror,
walk away, and two minutes later have no idea who they are, what they
look like. But whoever catches a glimpse of the revealed counsel of God —
the free life!—even out of the corner of his eye, and sticks with it,
is no distracted scatterbrain but a man or woman of action.
That person will find delight and affirmation in the action.

JAMES 1:19,22-25

May I make a bit of a confession?

In September 1998, I (Wes) was on my way to Seattle to be with friends who had recently lost a young adult daughter. My wife and I pledged that we'd be with them as often as possible in the months following this tragic event.

Scooting into my window seat on the plane, I was talking on my cell phone, telling someone else the reason for this trip. Not long into the flight, the man in the aisle seat began engaging me in conversation, confessing that he'd overheard the story of our friend's loss.

That began a four-and-a-half-year conversation with this man who had been born and raised in the United Kingdom. Here's my confession. As I got to know him, he stated that he had no

business for God or any religious people. I could halfway agree with him. I regularly do business with God, but I, too, don't always like hanging around religious people. It wasn't until late in 2000 during one of the breakfasts we had every three to six weeks that I fessed up to being an ordained minister. It took a year and a half of listening to this man's story to know when the time was ripe to begin sharing the gospel carefully and in doses he could swallow.[1]

Because I listened often—much more than trying to figure out what to say next to my friend Ken—he kept asking questions that eventually led him right into the kingdom. He died February 17, 2003, in an avalanche in the Colorado mountains. But because I listened, I know he's home. What a lesson this short relationship was for me. One of the last things Ken said to me was, "I've wanted to keep our friendship alive because no one has asked the questions you have; no one has listened to me more. Our times together have been leading me to places I never thought I'd go."

Praise be to God.

Here's the point of my story: We sometimes hear people like Ken say, "Don't preach to me," or we hear others apologize by saying, "Sorry, I didn't mean to preach at you." Have you noticed that the word *preach* has taken on a negative connotation in our society?

What does this mean for those of us who spend a good deal of time studying and gearing up for a weekly sermon or two? What does it say about those of us who've been called to preach the good news?

Certainly, many people can't stand preaching because they don't want to hear the Word of God. They want to run their own lives and not submit to the lordship of Jesus Christ. This is not exclusive to our society today. Some people didn't like Jesus'

preaching either, and they refused to listen to him.

But there are reasons why *preaching* has taken on a negative connotation in general today. Let's consider a few of those.

First, think about the concept of authority. People don't see preaching as just preaching; they see it as "preaching down" to them. Too much preaching can indicate an air of authority and moral superiority. We've all heard someone speak with that tone of voice or diction that just doesn't seem real. Some styles of preaching seem slick or overpolished. People can sense when our preaching is authentic—from the heart, from life lessons we've learned—and when it isn't.

When was the last time you listened to your own speaking? Listen to tapes of your messages with regularity to see if you're stirred by what God is saying to and through you. When was the last time you were confident enough—and eager enough to grow—to ask several others to critique your speaking? When was the last time you took a course to improve your speaking ability—not with the goal of being spectacular, but desiring to be the "real deal" before your congregation?[2]

Second, consider what we might call "guilt preaching." This is preaching the law without grace, preaching condemnation without forgiveness. This category could also include sermons that pressure people into service, commitment, or stewardship by making them feel guilty. Most of us know when we're preaching like this—when we're trying to be the "fourth person of the Trinity" and convince people of our position. This category also includes sermons that are against things (and we do need to be against *some* things). But sometimes we spend so much time developing what we're against that we never get around to speaking positively about what we're for. If all we do is feed our people sermons like these, we'll develop cranky, critical people. Our flocks will become just like us!

A third preaching problem is speaking without relevance. It's speaking without listening to the concerns of our church. It's monologue instead of dialogue. This style of preaching causes the people in our congregation to say, "Don't just preach to me. Listen to me."

You may either love or not care for the liturgy of the Anglican or Episcopal Church. Its beauty, though, is that every Sunday around the globe—in small to large and liberal to conservative parishes—a historical sense of togetherness occurs as these churches proclaim the good news from the *Book of Common Prayer.* Based on Scripture, this book that binds them together and creates dialogue can be used in some extraordinary ways if people slow down and ponder the recitations, the prayers, the affirmations, and the biblical injunctions.

What if on some Sunday (or whatever day you meet in this new world of ours), you simply, slowly, with passion read one of Paul's letters, as if he had just sent it to your congregation?[3] Your "preaching" would fall by the wayside and relevance would emerge.

Because Christendom lost the sense of mission found in the early church, the focus of the church began to center around the *event* of worship. The remnants of this shift still linger today.

Of course, exceptions exist in newer churches led by younger, life-hungry, evangelical leaders who understand the "ancient future" thoughts about being a church. But by and large, churches still cram the actual practice of most of the purposes of the church into the event we call a worship service.

Attracting those defined as "lost" is done there. Evangelism takes place there. Teaching occurs there. Getting a "spiritual high" happens there. For many, the only fellowship they have is

found there—sitting side by side, facing the same direction.

The focus of the week usually isn't an outreach project or act of service within our community, such as joining with others to build a home for Habitat for Humanity. We don't think of that as "church." Church means meeting together for worship—the Sunday production—and taking in the content and delivery of the sermon.

The people in the pews or chairs assess church to be good or bad, uplifting or depressing, based on how the preacher performs in the pulpit. As pastors, we believe we're successful if we pull off another stellar preaching performance. Of course, if we think that way, it means we want the people to be there for us—instead of us being there for the people and, foremost, for God.

Do we really believe that God is the audience at our worship? If we truly believed worship was for God, what would change within us and our congregations as we worship together before him?

We need to go back to the early apostolic model in order to help us rethink church. We think of church as what happens within the walls of the church building, but the apostolic model shows a way to do church without buildings.

Imagine that! This model has a lot to do with listening, something we can do anywhere.

First, we must listen to the Lord. One good friend calls this "eavesdropping on the Trinity." We listen to what God is saying through his Word and what he's saying through others who are seeking him. I (Wes) miss my friend who died in the avalanche for many reasons; one is that I learned so much from listening to his thoughts and questions.

Through the time we take to listen to God's Word, we become overwhelmed with our Creator's great love for the world. We become reengaged with God, who's not willing that any should perish but that all should come to repentance (see 2 Peter 3:9). Consider this question: What if you didn't read another religious book for a whole year and focused only on the Bible? What would happen in and through your life and ministry?

By listening to the Word of God, we again hear the gospel of the kingdom. We see the great work of God for the redemption of the world. We come closer to a Savior who entered the world to pay the penalty for sin—a Savior who calls us to enter his reign through repentance and faith.

By listening to the truth of God, we reconnect with the mission that he calls us to. We learn that our purpose in life is far away from the worldly pursuits that often captivate our hearts. We return to our communities to do simple acts of kindness and service for the sake of Christ and his kingdom.

By listening to the story of God, we find our own place in the story. We see that we're part of the history of redemption. By listening, we find encouragement in times of great trial to remain faithful, in times of disobedience to find forgiveness, and in times of victory to celebrate the presence of God in our midst. By listening, we learn to walk by faith.

We need consistently to be better listeners. We must be open to God's Word and allow it to challenge and change us. We must always be wary of thinking that we know it all or that we have it all figured out. This kind of thinking is dangerous—not only to us, but also to the flocks we care for. We can't grow and mature unless we're constantly challenged, molded, and formed by the Word of God.

Second, we must listen to each other. We need to be willing to listen for the ways that the Holy Spirit is moving among the

people we minister to. This affirms the fact that the Holy Spirit was given to the community of faith—to everyone. By listening to one another, we're better able to discern what God is calling our churches to be and do. A core question is this: Are we willing to trust the Spirit who is alive in the members of our congregation?

Third, we must listen with renewed interest to the needs of the world. After all, the church exists for the world. We must have the ears to hear what the world is thinking and what the Spirit wants to say to the world. We must evaluate and analyze what's going on in the world so we can minister to people in a way that's relevant to them.

Isn't it amazing how willing Jesus was to be among people who needed him most, not just among the religious leaders of his day? Think of how often he got criticized for being with "those sinners." When was the last time you were criticized for such behavior? Maybe we need to go hang out at our local bar for a bit and listen to the people in our larger community.[4] We just may find Jesus there ahead of us.

Much of what's spoken in preaching is true. But is it relevant to the real needs of people in the world? People have real needs in addition to their felt needs. People have a real need to hear the gospel, see it in action, and experience it. They have a real need to commit their lives to Christ. They need to repent of sin and believe the gospel of the kingdom. They need to find their purpose in life by becoming dependent on their Creator. However, we need to listen to the people in the world so we have points of contact with them.

Have you been listening—or just preaching?

Our world holds a lot of despair, purposelessness, and hopelessness. As people chase after money, prestige, and power, they hide their problems pretty well. No one likes to talk about their problems, but they're there. If the events of 9/11

taught us anything, it's that the world needs hope.

If we make the intentional investment of listening to the world so that we might speak the truth in love, many in our congregations will do the same. We need this balance, as do the people we serve. Otherwise we might become a separatist community, existing only for our own self-preservation. Or we might become so ensconced in our own worldliness that we lose our message and mission to the world. We need to be carefully relevant without diluting the truth and succumbing to worldliness.

Thom Rainer puts it this way: "A church that totally disregards the needs of the unchurched will reach few, if any, for the kingdom. But a church that makes most of its decisions based on the perceived needs of the same group is in danger of losing its biblical identity."[5]

This is no easy task, but it's our calling. Remember that Jesus hung out with all types of worldly characters before he hung on a cross for us.

At least one other reason exists why we need to learn to listen to the world. We need the humility to listen so that we can allow the world to correct and reprove us.

It's easy to blow off the world's criticism. But before we simply set aside critical words about the church, we need to ask if what those outside the church are saying is true. Why *do* Christian leaders get relatively bad press? Why *are* people critical of the church? The words of the world are often more true than we're willing to admit.

If we're honest about it, we'll admit that we deserve this negativity toward the church. Too often, the church has been mean, judgmental, and hypocritical. We need to repent of these sins. The world has been pointing out our errors. Have we been listening?

Listening isn't an easy skill to gain. It takes practice. If you've ever seen shows like *Crossfire* on CNN, you know how irritating it can be when people constantly talk over one another in order to make their point (it can sound like some church board meetings). We all need to learn that the validity of our arguments isn't related to the volume of our voices or the length of our speeches. We need to make sure we listen during the interpersonal discussions we have with others instead of thinking about what we're going to say next. That's just loading our verbal guns, so to speak.

As part of the community of faith, we need to be different. We need to be willing to take the time to listen to the Lord, to others, and to the world. This will make a significant difference in the mission we have to the world and in our churches— whatever size they are.

---

[1] Easily the best book we've read in a long time with regard to sharing the gospel is Brian McLaren, *More Ready Than You Realize: Evangelism As Dance in the Postmodern Matrix* (Grand Rapids, Mich.: Zondervan, 2002).

[2] We know of no better program than Ken Davis's Dynamic Communicators Workshop to improve your speaking gifts. Find out more at www.kendavis.com. We've both participated in this life-changing event, and those who hear us are glad we did.

[3] If you accept the dare to do this, read from *The Message*. This paraphrase, in part, was written for just such an opportunity.

[4] We're not really advocating barhopping. The point is this: Are you out among all the diverse groups of your community?

[5] Thom S. Rainer, *Surprising Insights from the Unchurched and Proven Ways to Reach Them* (Grand Rapids, Mich.: Zondervan, 2001) p. 89.

It's About Love—
Not Being Right

If I speak with human eloquence and angelic ecstasy but don't love,
I'm nothing but the creaking of a rusty gate.

If I speak God's Word with power, revealing all his mysteries and making
everything plain as day, and if I have faith that says to a mountain,
"Jump," and it jumps, but I don't love, I'm nothing.

If I give everything I own to the poor and even go to the stake to
be burned as a martyr, but I don't love, I've gotten nowhere.
So, no matter what I say, what I believe, and what I do,
I'm bankrupt without love.

1 CORINTHIANS 13:1-3

We can be right and still be wrong.

There's a town in New Jersey that received its name from a church dispute. The town is named Locktown because years ago during a church quarrel, officials locked the pastor out of the church. I don't know what the dispute was about or how serious the matter was. But to this day, by its name, the town still refers to that incident. Isn't it sad that a town could take its identity from a church fight?

Our churches can have the purest doctrine and the best Bible teaching—and still get it wrong. We can have the most logical method of apologetics and the best evangelism program—and still be wrong. We need to take seriously Paul's

words in 1 Corinthians 13. Our theology, our arguments, and our programs are empty without love.

The world is watching.

Have you ever wondered how your own attitude and the attitude of your congregation affect your church's reputation in the town where you're trying to proclaim the gospel? It seems that many of us are blind to what the people of our communities think of us. Worse, we don't even care what they think, as long as we have the truth.

The world has seen too many petty disputes over nonessential doctrines. They've watched venom spew from our lips against each other. They've seen churches split over the most insignificant matters. They've witnessed how we treat one another with disrespect and ridicule and then go back to our churches to sing "Blest Be the Tie That Binds." They've seen the way we work against each other while claiming to believe a creed that speaks of "the communion of saints." The world sees all of this as hypocrisy, and they're not wrong.

A few weeks ago I (Glenn) had the privilege of listening to an African-American pastor speak personally about the prejudice he'd endured growing up in America. He spoke of the hatred he'd faced during his college years and the bigotry he'd suffered in the profession of medicine. It was especially painful to see his expression as he spoke with tears in his eyes of the prejudice that he'd faced within the church. Such prejudice is not only a failure to love, but also a failure to stand up for the truth of the kingdom—a kingdom composed of people from every gender, nation, tribe, language, and ethnic group.

In one of his epistles, Paul writes to the younger Timothy, "I'm writing this letter so you'll know how things ought to go in God's household, this God-alive church, bastion of truth" (1 Timothy 3:14-15). Can we keep learning to speak the truth in love? Can we disagree with one another with respect? Can we learn to "make every effort to keep the unity of the Spirit through the bond of peace" (Ephesians 4:3, NIV)? Doesn't even the way that we disagree with each other matter for the sake of the mission of God's kingdom?

The people around us that we're commissioned to reach with the gospel need to hear more than the truth of Christianity. They've often heard the truth from us. However, they remained unconvinced because they haven't seen the evidence of that truth lived out in our lives.

The people we serve need more than propositional truth. They need to see the goodness of Christianity—the goodness of truth expressed in deeds of love and mercy, goodness expressed in patience and kindness, sacrificial goodness, a goodness that even demonstrates a love for our enemies. Unless the people we serve—inside and outside our churches—see goodness, they won't come to see the truth.

We need to consistently examine ourselves. How true is our Christianity if it's not good? Simply being right isn't enough.

There was a time when the church, though outlawed, persecuted, and misunderstood, was known for its life-transforming love. Henry Chadwick writes of this love, which brought success to the early Christian church:

> The practical application of charity was probably the
> most potent single cause of Christian success. The
> pagan comment "see how they love one another"
> (reported by Tertullian) was not irony. Christian charity

expressed itself in the care of the poor, for widows and orphans, in visits to brethren in prison or condemned to the living death of labour in the mines, and in social action in time of calamity like famine, earthquake, pestilence and war.[1]

The early Christians were so committed to caring for one another's needs that history records their practice of fasting to save food to give to others who were more in need.[2] What would happen if the world today could see such a clear and consistent demonstration of God's love? What would happen if we were seen as servants to our neighborhoods and communities instead of recruiters of new members? What would happen if the people within our congregations truly loved one another and learned to love our neighbors?

John the Revelator writes the words of God to the church of Ephesus that the *necessity to love* is a matter essential for our own existence:

Write this to Ephesus, to the Angel of the church. The One with Seven Stars in his right-fist grip, striding through the golden seven-lights' circle, speaks:

"I see what you've done, your hard, hard work, your refusal to quit. I know you can't stomach evil, that you weed out apostolic pretenders. I know your persistence, your courage in my cause, that you never wear out.

"But you walked away from your first love—why? What's going on with you, anyway? Do you have any idea how far you've fallen? A Lucifer fall!

"Turn back! Recover your dear early love. No time to waste, for I'm well on my way to removing your light from the golden circle.

"You do have this to your credit: You hate the Nicolaitan business. I hate it, too.

"Are your ears awake? Listen. Listen to the Wind Words, the Spirit blowing through the churches. I'm about to call each conqueror to dinner. I'm spreading a banquet of Tree-of-Life fruit, a supper plucked from God's orchard." (Revelation 2:1-7)

Certainly, the church of Ephesus was doctrinally sound. The apostle Paul labored there for years. Timothy had ministered there for a while, during which time Paul wrote him two letters. Many years later, in A.D. 431, the Ecumenical Council of the Church held in Ephesus dealt with the false teachings of Nestorius and Pelagius.

Surely, this church had its doctrine together. They'd tested false apostles and taken a stand against the practices of the Nicolaitans. Still they made a serious, life-threatening error. They'd forsaken love—an error that put their very survival at risk. The Lord called them to repentance.

The same Spirit of God is speaking these words to us today. Don't we also forsake the weightier matters of the law—to love the Lord our God with all of our hearts and to love our neighbors as ourselves?

This matter can't be overstated. The way we demonstrate the love of Christ has supreme significance with regard to our calling in the world—the mission of God, the proclamation of the gospel of the kingdom. Jesus said that this would be our defining characteristic: "This is how everyone will recognize that you are my disciples—when they see the love you have for each other" (John 13:35).

Love calls us out of our selfishness and personal ambition to look beyond ourselves to others. Loving others calls us to be merciful, forgiving, and kind. It demands that we be sacrificial of our time, talents, and possessions. Love is difficult. It's often dirty. It can be dangerous and discouraging.

It takes time to love. It takes an investment of time and a commitment to develop relationships. We're not always willing to make such an investment, especially if we have goals or an agenda in mind. When we're honest, we don't think we can take the time or energy to make such a sacrifice. We falsely assume that we have more important things to do.

Love is difficult for many reasons. Some people are just hard to love. They can overwhelm us with their neediness or dysfunctions. They can be cantankerous or unaccepting of our love. They may never be grateful.

Love is often dirty. It requires that we do things we don't want to do—to get our hands dirty being a servant to others. One summer I (Glenn) took a brief break from my regular schedule to join other members of our church in painting a house for a missionary we support. As they held a paintbrush in their hands, some of the men who labored with me on this project expressed the fact that they hate to paint. One said he'd never do this at his own house; he'd hire someone else to do it. But there they were, scraping old paint and applying new.

That's love. It's dirty, and it calls us to move outside our comfort zones. When the missionary woman who owns the house asked why we volunteered to do this work for her, the answer was simple: Jesus calls us to love one another. Jesus washed his disciple's feet, and he calls us to follow his example. Sometimes we wash with paint.

Pastoral ministry is a messy business. People get tangled up in sin and carried off into nasty places. Let's not have an idyllic

notion of what it means to be a shepherd. The reality is that caring for sheep can be really messy. If we're going to minister in the name of Jesus, then we're going to deal with the prostitutes, tax collectors, and sinners of our day.

Sometimes we find that those "sinners" have been sitting in our pews and listening to our preaching for years. Still, love calls us to enter into the tangled messes of their lives to minister the hope of the gospel. This is the incarnational ministry that Jesus calls us to.

Love is dangerous. It's a risky business that requires a certain vulnerability and transparency. In pastoral ministry we're often not willing to let down our guard. We're more concerned with maintaining power and status or keeping up a "pastoral image."

Love is dangerous because it sometimes calls us to step into the middle of a controversy to make peace. This can leave us vulnerable to the possibility of being misunderstood, becoming a scapegoat, and bearing anger and resentment from all sides.

Yes, love is dangerous. It was dangerous love that nailed Jesus to the cross.

Love can be discouraging. How often have you poured your life into other people, only to see them walk away—either to go to another church or perhaps even to leave the faith altogether. When we're weary, it's easy to develop an attitude that turns our hearts away from love. It's far safer to project a professional persona and stay aloof. As one friend said many years ago, "It doesn't pay to be bighearted—it only gives people more room to stab you."

Indeed, some of us who've chosen to be vulnerable have found our openness used against us. Perhaps because of this, we've developed a safer strategy. But "safety" is not a strategy of love.

Because love is difficult, dangerous, and discouraging, it's easy to look for some substitute that can replace the time- and energy-consuming call to love. Maybe we turn to the rightness of doctrine or the rightness of our cause. That's when we exchange being right for being loving.

Not only do we see this lack of love within the church, but we also find a similar deficiency in our relationships to the world. If we're honest with ourselves, how often do we judge and criticize our neighbors for not meeting up to our standards, rather than just loving them? We preach to them the rightness of our cause with all of the accompanying right doctrine, but where are the deeds of love and mercy? If we minister in the name of Jesus, we're also called to be a friend of sinners.

How good a friend to sinners are you? How often are you at their places for a meal? Are you getting to know them on their turfs or always expecting them to be on yours? How generous are you with sinners? In what ways do you love them, no matter what?

In giving us the Great Commandment, Jesus says that all the Law and Prophets are summed up in the commands to love the Lord our God with all of our being and to love our neighbors as ourselves (see Matthew 22:37-39). We need to ask ourselves if this is the reputation we have in our communities.

Do the people in our towns recognize us as people and as a church who love God with all of our hearts and love our neighbors as ourselves? We've studied and learned the Great Commandment in a theoretical way. But has it passionately captivated us to the extent that it's become our practice—our way of life?

As we've intentionally mentioned several times, much of the state of contemporary Christianity has to do with our acceptance of

modernism. While we don't like to admit it, this has had a profound effect on us. Modernism is so deeply ingrained in us that we're often unable to see what it's done to us.

Christianity—whether we like to admit it or not—has in too many places become logically tight, mean-spirited, and judgmental. Evangelism is a matter of "closing the deal" with a quick presentation and prayer, rather than the hard work of serving the community with love and self-sacrifice and building relationships with people who don't yet know the Lord. Our evangelism practices don't reflect the patience of waiting on God.

Brian McLaren writes of this in his most refreshing book on the subject of evangelism:

On the street, evangelism is equated with pressure. It means selling God as if God were vinyl siding, replacement windows, or a mortgage refinancing service. It means shoving your ideas down someone's throat, threatening him with hell if he does not capitulate to your logic or Scripture quoting. It means excluding everyone from God's grace except those who agree with the evangelizer (a.k.a. evangelist). When preceded by the word *television,* the word *evangelism* grows even darker and more sinister—sleazy even. It means rehearsed, mechanical monologues, sales pitches, spiels, unrequested sermons or lectures, crocodile tears, uncomfortable confrontations sometimes made worse by Nutrasweet smiles and overdone eye contact and too-sincere professions of love for one's soul and concern for one's eternal destiny. ("Yeah, right. The truth is, you're trying to get more human fuel for your religious machinery—another convert, another notch in the belt, another victory for your ideology.")[3]

Because the church adopted principles of modernism, we haven't been faithful to the gospel of the kingdom—a gospel that calls the church to be salt, light, and a city on a hill. We often care more about converts than about people. We concentrate on recruiting rather than disciple making. We argue and debate, picket and protest. But does anyone see our good works and give praise to our Father in heaven?

We've called for it many times, but we'll encourage it again here: We must return to the much older ways. The methods of doing what we do as the community of God's people must become more like the apostolic model. In terms of our place in history, we're much closer to this than we realize.

The place of mission today is no longer out on the edges of the empire. It's right outside the front doors of our church buildings. We need to keep our eyes wide open and see that the fields ready for harvest are right next door.

What are we doing about reaching the people of our localities with the gospel of Jesus—and not just in the "same old, same old" ways? How can our churches, no matter the size, demonstrate the love of God to our neighbors in ways that don't reek of recruitment but rather demonstrate our real concern for them? How can we love our neighbors into the kingdom?

Does the whole world need to know? Of course. We're not suggesting that foreign missions don't have value. But this is a plea suggesting that we first need to wake up to the world outside our doors and within our immediate communities. People should be able to look at the church and see what it's like to live under the reign of God. They ought to be able to sense something of the *shalom,* the well-being, of God's reign being lived out among them. The people of our day need more than tight, logical arguments and proof. They need to see a demonstration of the kingdom lived out before them so that they might see, experience, and enter it.

This chapter comes to an end with a few words to pastors and church leaders about our calling to love the sheep. Jesus says that he, as the Good Shepherd, lays down his life for the sheep (see John 10:11). Jesus serves as an example of how to minister to the flock of God.

We must also lay down our lives for our sheep. The apostle John wrote, "This is how we know what love is: Jesus Christ laid down his life for us. And we ought to lay down our lives for our brothers" (1 John 3:16, NIV). Certainly this must be a way of life for those of us who are called to serve as pastors to God's flocks.

As a pastor, you have a choice. You can choose to impress people or to influence them. You can try to live above the people you serve, or you can live with and among them. Sure, you can probably impress some people with your education and degrees, your ability to handle the original languages of the Bible, or your abilities to counsel or preach. But you can make a better choice. Put aside the theological jargon and titles and simply speak the truth in love. Let love permeate your relationships and demonstrate that you really, sincerely care about the sheep of your whole community.

When we look at Jesus' life, it's easy to see his potential to impress people. According to the biblical record of the miracles he performed, he certainly did impress others. But the Gospels also speak about times when he didn't seem to impress anyone.

While in Nazareth, he was known simply as Mary and Joseph's son. Although he had the ability to impress Herod, he chose not to. He often told the people whom he healed not to tell others about it. He was born into a humble carpenter's family and lived much of his life as a homeless man. He was despised and rejected. He knew the emotion of grief. Most

people couldn't see beyond the Incarnation to behold his glory.

Jesus didn't always impress, but he always had influence. He is our model for what it means to be a shepherd. His example points to a great difference between true shepherds and rent-a-shepherd hirelings. True shepherds have an investment in the sheep. They are called to pay a cost, to make an investment of life that not all are willing to make. True shepherds know that shepherding isn't a task for the faint of heart.

True shepherds understand what it means to have a shepherd's heart. These shepherds know their sheep and are more concerned about the sheep than saving their own skin. True shepherds are willing to bear the scars, the disappointments, and the hardships of the task because they care deeply for their sheep. One thing is true if we're going to shepherd our flocks like Jesus: It's about love.

---

[1] Henry Chadwick, *The Early Church,* rev. ed. (London: Penguin Books, 1993), p. 56.

[2] For a mention of this practice in the early church, as well as other acts of mercy, see Igino Giordani, *The Social Message of the Early Church Fathers* (Patterson, N.J.: St. Anthony's Guild, 1944), p. 307.

[3] Brian McLaren, *More Ready Than You Realize: Evangelism As Dance in the Postmodern Matrix* (Grand Rapids, Mich.: Zondervan, 2002), pp. 12-13.

It's About Our Triune God—
Not Us

Do you want to be counted wise, to build a reputation for wisdom?
Here's what you do: Live well, live wisely, live humbly. It's the way you live,
not the way you talk, that counts. Mean-spirited ambition isn't wisdom.
Boasting that you are wise isn't wisdom. Twisting the truth to make
yourselves sound wise isn't wisdom. It's the furthest thing from wisdom—
it's animal cunning, devilish conniving. Whenever you're trying to look
better than others or get the better of others, things fall apart
and everyone ends up at the others' throats.

JAMES 3:13-16

He was a man I (Wes) had looked forward to meeting. I'd heard much about him, read some of what he'd written, and known people who'd been influenced by his writing ministry. But the writer and the speaker turned out to be two entirely different people in the same body.

As I sat with several others who'd also looked forward to a time of lively and interactive discussion around a good meal, I was dismayed at how this man dominated the entire conversation. Whenever anyone spoke, he would one-up the person with his own story. He never asked anyone a question, and with great skill he avoided answering any questions we tried to ask. After about thirty minutes, I was in a weird kind of awe with how one person could eat, drink, and talk so much without taking a breath. He went on and on about how incredible and necessary

he and his ministry had become in recent years.

I realize that I'm a little twisted in some ways, but I became intrigued about when this man would ever take a breath. Over the course of the evening, my emotions went from amazement, to humor, to pity for this man who just kept eating, drinking, and talking about himself and his ministry for almost two hours. At the end of the evening he said, "Look for my next book. It will be out in a month, and it's the best one I've written. I've got two more in the works—you should get them when they come out." With that, he stood up, bid us good night, and walked to his hotel room.

The next day he and I rode down in an elevator together for a general session of the conference we were attending. He looked right at me as if he'd never seen me before and didn't say a word until we got off. Then he told me his name (as if I didn't know) and said, "I'm going to go do a book signing. Buy one of my books and bring it into the display area, and I'll sign it for you. It's the best book you'll buy here this week." Confession time: I don't own any of his books.

Certainly, we all have our flaws. Ministry is for flawed people just like you and me—and that man. But as humorist Garrison Keillor would say about some of the folks in Lake Wobegon, "That man was too full of himself." It got me to wondering, *Where am I too full of myself? Where does my "I" work overtime to get the glory that truly belongs to God?*

Envy. Selfish ambition. These things seem so wise in the eyes of the world. They're the ways of the world—to get things done and make your mark. These sins creep into our hearts so subtly that we may not even know they're there. They come disguised in a cloak of spirituality.

We want to reach those we've defined as "the lost." We want to make a difference for Jesus. We care about building the kingdom. So we push and pull and strive. We claim that we only

want to do something for Jesus. But in our hearts we know the truth. The truth is, we long to be someone in the eyes of our peers. We want to be acknowledged and respected. We hope to make our mark in church history, even if it's only a footnote. Or we seek that proverbial fifteen minutes of fame.

Pastoring a smaller church is tough, precisely because of this battle that we have in our hearts—the battle to make our mark in the world and before our peers and families. And because so many of us have bought into the value structure of the world, it becomes more and more difficult to believe that pastoring a smaller congregation is doing something significant.

But what if we use a different assessment from the prevailing one in which success is based on attendance figures, dynamic programs, growing budgets, and expanded facilities? What if we use an assessment we've discussed several times—one that has little or nothing to do with any of these human measurements? What if faithfulness to God's calling on our life is all that really matters—no matter what size church God has placed us in?

Lesslie Newbigin rightly reminds us that "mission in Christ's way will not be a success story as the world reckons success. There is a kind of ideology of success that fits badly with the gospel."[1]

You may be thinking, *You're making a false dichotomy. The Bible calls us to both faithfulness and fruitfulness.* Yes, the Bible calls us to both. But we're questioning how these matters should be defined and measured. We can look to Newbigin for some answers:

> Success in the sense of growth in the number of commit-
> ted Christians is not in our hands. It is the work of the
> Holy Spirit to call men and women to faith in Jesus, and
> the Spirit does so in ways that are often mysterious and
> beyond any possibility of manipulation or even of com-
> prehension by us. What is required of us is faithfulness

in word and deed, at whatever the cost; faithfulness in
action for truth, for justice, for mercy, for compassion;
faithfulness in speaking the name of Jesus when the time
is right, bearing witness, by explicit word as occasion
arises, to God whose we are and whom we serve. There
are situations where the word is easy and the deed is
costly; there are situations where the deed is easy and
the word is costly. Whether in word or in deed, what is
required in every situation is that we be faithful to him
who said to his disciples: "As the Father sent me, so I
send you," and showed them his hands and his side.[2]

As we continue to learn to assess success according to
Scripture, we'll see that numbers aren't as important as the grit of
sticking with the calling God gives us. Wherever we're serving
our Lord, we need to be about living a life of fruitfulness that
invites others to follow Jesus.

Perhaps we need a new concept for our contemporary
heroes—men and women who labor faithfully despite the seeming
success of the world, men and women who labor in ministry in
Christ's way. Maybe our heroes should be those who've had the
opportunity to move on to bigger congregations and better situations
but have chosen instead to stay where the Lord has called them.

If you're one of these pastors, thank you for your faithfulness. Thank you for all that you do, endure, and model. You're
not a loser—far from it! You show the rest of us the way, the
truth, and the life we're all called to live.

Somehow, we must learn to measure success in terms of being
and making disciples. Are the varying kinds of people in our

congregations growing in spiritual maturity? Are they learning more and more what it authentically means to deny themselves and follow Jesus?

Once again, we come face-to-face with the dilution of the gospel that has taken place in contemporary evangelicalism. We've been offering a gospel that speaks of personal salvation, escape from hell, and the gift of eternal life. But that just makes Christianity a tool for more comfortable living.

Instead, we need to remember that the gospel isn't about us; it's about God and his glory. The gospel is the gospel of the kingdom. The gospel that Jesus taught and that we find in the pages of the New Testament is a gospel that calls us to live under the reign of God. It's a gospel that demands repentance. It's a gospel that requires a change of mind to produce a transformed life. There's no salvation apart from the lordship of Jesus Christ. If Jesus isn't our Lord, he won't be our Savior.

There's another part of the gospel that we can't separate ourselves from—the part about living under Christ's rule. This is the part that demands discipleship, that calls us to find our identity in Christ, that calls us to daily die to ourselves so that we no longer live for ourselves but live instead for Christ. This is the good news that God's kingdom has come—the good news that sinners like us, who've forfeited all rights to God's blessings, can inherit his kingdom by living in submission to the reigning King. Are we still passionate and grateful for this aspect of our relationship with him? We need to consistently, sincerely, and humbly model it for those we've been called to serve and shepherd.

This message isn't very popular in our consumer-driven, individualistic culture. Most of us are more concerned about what God can do for us rather than what he requires of us. It's easy to lose the awe of our relationship with him.

In our day, it's probably easier to draw a crowd when we

offer the gospel in terms of a self-help message on how life can work better. When we claim to have a formula for making life easier or more manageable, we can get people to listen. It's far more difficult to maintain a crowd when we get courageous and tell people they must sacrifice, deny their own demands for life, and follow Jesus, whether life is working out for them or not. But no matter how we try to present our message, no other gospel exists than the gospel of the kingdom.

We're called to be faithful to this gospel. We're called to be fruitful. To return to the much older ways, we must reengage with the gospel of the kingdom. A false gospel that adds benefits and ease to our lives but costs nothing isn't found in the pages of Scripture. It would be a gospel of cheap grace.

Søren Kierkegaard notes:

Imagine a kind of medicine that possesses in full dosage a laxative effect but in half dose a constipating effect. Suppose someone is suffering from constipation. But— for some reason or other, perhaps there is not enough for a full dose or because it is feared that such a large amount might be too much—in order to do something, he is given, with the best of intentions, a half dose: "After all, it is at least something." What a tragedy!

So it is with today's Christianity. . . . But we Christians go on practicing this well-intentioned half-hearted act from generation to generation. We produce Christians by the millions, are proud of it—yet have no inkling that we are doing just the opposite of what we intend to do. . . .

The greatest danger to Christianity is, I contend, not heresies, heterodoxies, not atheists, not profane secularism—no, but the kind of orthodoxy which is cordial drivel, mediocrity served up sweet. . . . The very essence

of Christianity is utterly opposed to this mediocrity. . . .

Today's orthodoxy essentially has its abode in the cordial drivel of family life. This is utterly dangerous to Christianity. Christianity does not oppose debauchery and uncontrollable passions and the like as much as it is opposes this flat mediocrity, this nauseating atmosphere, this homey, civil togetherness, where admittedly great crimes, wild excesses, and powerful aberrations cannot easily occur—but where God's unconditional demand has even greater difficulty in accomplishing what it requires: the majestic obedience of submission.[3]

If we're going to return to the much older ways, we have to throw off the mediocrity of Christendom. We have to relearn the necessity of discipleship. We need to be more free to declare the gospel of the kingdom. Jesus came to set the captives free. May we commit to living in his great gift of grace and freedom, and may we lead those in our churches to that same freedom.

It might help us recapture the much older ways if we get a glimpse of the big picture. Let's think about the history of the church and our place in it. To help us with this perspective, consider these words from Martin Luther:

It is not we who can sustain the church, nor was it those who came before us, nor will it be those who come after us. It was, and is, and will be, the one who says: "I am with you always, even to the end of time."

As it says in Hebrews 13: "Jesus Christ, the same *yesterday, today,* and *for ever.*" And in Revelation 1:

"Who was, and *is,* and *is to come."* Truly he is that one, and no one else is, or ever can be.

For you and I were not alive thousands of years ago, yet the church was sustained without us—and it was done by the one of whom it says, "Who was," and "Yesterday." . . . The church would perish before our very eyes, and we along with it (as we daily prove), were it not for that other man who so obviously upholds the church and us.

This we can lay hold of and feel, even though we are reluctant to believe it. We must give ourselves to the one of whom it is said: "Who is," and "Today."

Again, we can do nothing to sustain the church when we are dead. But he will do it, of whom it is said: *"Who is to come,"* and *"For ever."*[4]

Luther reminds us that the church was here long before we arrived on the scene. Pending the Lord's return, it will be here long after we're gone.

We stand in a long line of people—those who've gone on before us and those who will remain faithful after us. God is in control of this history. Christ is the meaning of all of this. He's the purpose, the goal. He'll sustain his church until the day he returns to restore the world and make all things new.

Our hope isn't in our accomplishments or in finding success in the church business. Our hope is in Christ, who gives our present life meaning and purpose by calling us to serve him. He promises to return for his bride. That's us! No matter how we live, our treasure is reserved in heaven for us. On this planet we live like Abraham—never being able to settle down because we're looking for a heavenly city that God has prepared for us.

As a pastor, your calling is all about the Lord. Your calling

isn't about you. Instead of trying to make a name for yourself, you're called to honor Christ—to live for him with everything that you are and everything that you're not. You're called to labor faithfully in the present with a hope for the future.

Your confidence isn't found in the work of your hands or in the latest fad that promises success. Your confidence is in Christ, who'll continue to preserve his church until he returns to take her home.

As a leader in the church of Jesus, if you're going to be used of the Lord to move into the much older ways, then you must first of all be a disciple of Jesus. Jesus says that to be his disciple, you must give up your own life. You must die to your own dreams and ambitions in order to live for him.

You won't find significance by carving out a special place of importance for yourself or by making a name for yourself. Instead you'll find true significance by being a servant of the Lord Most High—wherever *he* puts you. You must set your heart on honoring the Lord, not seeking honor for yourself.

As a wholehearted Christ-follower, you'll put aside the notion of massaging your career into important places. As a disciple, you'll want to surrender the desire to be looked upon as a professional. You'll have to trust the Lord instead of the latest techniques that show promise for success in the church business.

For you to be a disciple and a God-glorifying leader in his church, you must be willing to be a servant. You'll seek the Lord to develop in you the fruit of the Spirit. You'll die to the busyness of seeking after achievement in order to allow the Lord to bear fruit in you. You'll become more and more God-dependent and put aside mere strategizing in order to follow the Spirit. You'll proclaim the whole gospel of the kingdom by both word and deed.

Recognizing that it's *really* all about Jesus means acknowledging that it's all about the Cross. The Cross that Jesus refused to reject must become a way of life for you. As Dietrich Bonhoeffer clearly reminds us, "When Christ calls a man, he bids him come and die."[5]

This is hard to say and still harder to live, but being a disciple of Jesus means that you're willing to give up your life, dreams, and ambitions to simply be a servant—a servant of Jesus Christ. This doesn't mean that you'll have no life, dreams, or energy to do God's bidding. But the submission of daily giving up your life and taking up his cross is what following Jesus is all about. That's the gospel truth.

Realistically, authentically, it's not about getting a better position. It's not about a bigger salary, more perks, or greater prestige. It's not about finding a formula that makes life work. It's not about being touted as a pastor of one of the top-ten growing churches in the world. It's not about maintaining professional status. It's not about us—it's all about Jesus!

As a leader in the church, you must pave the way with this attitude about life. You must lead by example. You must die to stay where the Lord has placed you—this place with all of its aggravating difficulties. You must die if you're to leave someplace where you're comfortable and familiar to go to some other field where God is calling you. Discipleship is about fulfilling the calling of the Lord. That's still his original intent.

Where has the Lord placed you?

Are you, like Jeremiah, in a place where only a few people seem to listen? Is it a place where you're constantly behind in the budget, where the facilities don't ever seem up to par, or where you're the brunt of constant criticism? Is it a place where you feel

as though you're constantly hitting your head against a wall?

When we see examples of God's servants in the Bible, why should we expect things to be any different? How can we look to the prophets and other faithful people and hold them up as great heroes and examples if we're unwilling to follow in their steps?

Abraham endured fears and threats as a stranger in a foreign land. The apostle Paul endured riots, beatings, stonings, imprisonment, and shipwrecks. Moses endured constant criticism and uprisings. He persevered through times when the people would not follow in faith. He dealt with many disappointments. Moses' own brother, who knew better, led the people of Israel in worshiping a golden calf. Most of the prophets remained faithful in times when no one seemed to listen to them.

And let us never forget Jesus, who showed us the scars on his hands, his feet, his side. He did this as a reminder of the way to do ministry in the world: "As the Father has sent me, I am sending you" (John 20:21, NIV). Dietrich Bonhoeffer wrote, "To endure the cross is not a tragedy; it is the suffering which is the fruit of an exclusive allegiance to Jesus Christ. When it comes, it is not an accident, but a necessity."[6]

You don't exist for yourself. Your purpose in life isn't to win the acceptance of your peers or the acclaim of the world. You exist for Jesus. Jesus is Lord—you're not. He calls the shots in your life—you don't.

This sentiment is captured in words from the *Trinity Hymnal:*

Father, I know that all my life
Is portioned out for me;
The changes that are sure to come,
I do not fear to see:
I ask thee for a present mind,
Intent on pleasing thee.

I ask thee for the daily strength,
To none that ask denied,
A mind to blend with outward life,
While keeping at thy side,
Content to fill a little space,
If thou be glorified.[7]

The long history of Christendom has given us a set of expectations we've grown comfortable with. They match the expectations that have become a part of our culture. But the Bible gives us a picture that's a far cry from the professional type of ministry that we've been trying to maintain.

As the world moves further away from the church, the church will become more and more marginalized. We can expect to lose our voice and power in the world. The signs of this breakdown are all around us. But that's not bad news. The good news is that we can expect to be molded by the hands of a Sovereign God and moved more and more toward his original intent for the church.

Are we ready to move into this future? Are we willing to go there? Will we, with bold confidence, trust the Lord to slay the giants in the land before us? Or will we, like the children of Israel so long ago, cower at the sights and the strangeness of this new territory, refuse to move forward, and in doing so, perish in the current wilderness?

It's possible to live in denial about the future of the church. We need to recognize the realities that are so clearly set before us.

No matter what size congregation you serve, let there be no doubt: The church *will* make it. The Lord's purposes aren't going to fail. You'll make it, not because of your strategizing or marketing

plans, not because of your latest programs or consumer-driven appeal. You'll make it because Jesus Christ, who is the same yesterday, today, and forever, will remain the head of the church. He'll preserve you and push you into this necessary future.

Daily these questions loom huge on the horizons of your ministry: Are you willing to say "yes" to the Lord? Are you following him and his ways? Will you remain curious and learn to rethink and retool for this future?

The Lord has great things in store for his church—but not great as the world counts greatness. Perhaps the greatest days in church history are still ahead of us. But we must be willing to become more of what our Lord has called us to be.

We'll have to lose our domestication and become wild again. We'll have to learn to live more and more by what Brennan Manning calls "ruthless trust"—trust in the Lord when the chips are down and the circumstances look bleak.

Perhaps those who labor in the more difficult fields of harvest are the most ready for this future. Perhaps from this group of men and women, the church will learn to move into the new land of marginality with the inner strength and faith needed for the journey—a journey where the church will recapture its authenticity, deny its worldliness, and learn again the great value of weakness.

Quiet now.

Take some time to ponder these final words. You may even want to make them a prayer of renewal to your calling. With one

heart and one mind, will you stand before our triune God and say with renewed hope and deeper conviction, "Oh, Lord, here am I, send me"?

Jesus hears your prayer. For just a moment, listen. He's still speaking to you:

> "God authorized and commanded me to commission you: Go out and train everyone you meet, far and near, in this way of life, marking them by baptism in the threefold name: Father, Son, and Holy Spirit. Then instruct them in the practice of all I have commanded you. I'll be with you as you do this, day after day after day, right up to the end of the age." (Matthew 28:18-20)

---

[1] Lesslie Newbigin, *Mission in Christ's Way: A Gift, a Command, an Assurance* (New York: Friendship Press, 1988) p. 13.

[2] Newbigin, p. 14.

[3] Charles E. Moore, ed., *Provocations: Spiritual Writings of Kierkegaard* (Farmingtom, Pa.: The Plough Publishing House of the Bruderhof Foundation, 1999), pp. 16-17.

[4] Martin Luther, quoted in Alister E. McGrath, *Luther's Theology of the Cross* (Oxford: Blackwell Publishers, Ltd., 1985), p. 181. Original emphasis recorded.

[5] Dietrich Bonhoeffer, *The Cost of Discipleship* (New York: Macmillan, 1977), p. 99.

[6] Bonhoeffer, p. 98.

[7] Originally published in Anna L. Waring, "Father, I know that all my life," *Hymns and Meditations* (1850); later published in *Hymns and Meditations* rev. ed. (London: Society for Promoting Christian Knowledge, 1911).

Epilogue

The apostle Paul's letter to the Christians in Colossae is familiar to most who have journeyed through these pages to the end of this book. As we ponder our place in the church of Jesus Christ in future days, we'd be wise to read thoughtfully Paul's words from Colossians. We conclude our writing with both a thankful and humble spirit that God invites us to share his good news—in his energy and power, for his honor and glory, now and forever more—in order to once more be of one heart and one mind with God's original intent for his church.

May your spirit soak in these words. Listen carefully. They're God's words for you—wherever you are, whoever you are—as his faithful servant.

Be encouraged.

The Message is as true among you today as when you first heard it. It doesn't diminish or weaken over time. It's the same all over the world. The Message bears fruit and gets larger and stronger, just as it has in you. From the very first day you heard and recognized the truth of what God is doing, you've been hungry for more. It's

as vigorous in you now as when you learned it from our friend and close associate Epaphras. He is one reliable worker for Christ! I could always depend on him. He's the one who told us how thoroughly love had been worked into your lives by the Spirit.

Be assured that from the first day we heard of you, we haven't stopped praying for you, asking God to give you wise minds and spirits attuned to his will, and so acquire a thorough understanding of the ways in which God works. We pray that you'll live well for the Master, making him proud of you as you work hard in his orchard. As you learn more and more how God works, you will learn how to do *your* work. We pray that you'll have the strength to stick it out over the long haul—not the grim strength of gritting your teeth but the glory-strength God gives. It is strength that endures the unendurable and spills over into joy, thanking the Father who makes us strong enough to take part in everything bright and beautiful that he has for us.

God rescued us from dead-end alleys and dark dungeons. He's set us up in the kingdom of the Son he loves so much, the Son who got us out of the pit we were in, got rid of the sins we were doomed to keep repeating.

We look at this Son and see the God who cannot be seen. We look at this Son and see God's original purpose in everything created. For everything, absolutely everything, above and below, visible and invisible, rank after rank after rank of angels—*everything* got started in him and finds its purpose in him. He was there before any of it came into existence and holds it all together right up to this moment. And when it comes to the

church, he organizes and holds it together, like a head
does a body.

He was supreme in the beginning and—leading the
resurrection parade—he is supreme in the end. From
beginning to end he's there, towering far above everything, everyone. So spacious is he, so roomy, that
everything of God finds its proper place in him without
crowding. Not only that, but all the broken and dislo-
cated pieces of the universe—people and things, ani-
mals and atoms—get properly fixed and fit together in
vibrant harmonies, all because of his death, his blood
that poured down from the Cross.

You yourselves are a case study of what he does. At
one time you all had your backs turned to God, thinking
rebellious thoughts of him, giving him trouble every
chance you got. But now, by giving himself completely
at the Cross, actually *dying* for you, Christ brought you
over to God's side and put your lives together, whole
and holy in his presence. You don't walk away from a
gift like that! You stay grounded and steady in that bond
of trust, constantly tuned in to the Message, careful not
to be distracted or diverted. There is no other Message—
just this one. Every creature under heaven gets this same
Message. I, Paul, am a messenger of this Message.

I want you to know how glad I am that it's me sitting here in this jail and not you. There's a lot of suffering to be entered into in this world—the kind of
suffering Christ takes on. I welcome the chance to take
my share in the church's part of that suffering. When I
became a servant in this church, I experienced this suffering as a sheer gift, God's way of helping me serve
you, laying out the whole truth.

This mystery has been kept in the dark for a long time, but now it's out in the open. God wanted everyone, not just Jews, to know this rich and glorious secret inside and out, regardless of their background, regardless of their religious standing. The mystery in a nutshell is just this: Christ is in you, therefore you can look forward to sharing in God's glory. It's that simple. That is the substance of our Message. We preach *Christ,* warning people not to add to the Message. We teach in a spirit of profound common sense so that we can bring each person to maturity. To be mature is to be basic. Christ! No more, no less. That's what I'm working so hard at day after day, year after year, doing my best with the energy God so generously gives me. (Colossians 1:5-29)

Resources

Books to encourage your heart, your mind, your relationships, your ministry:

Spencer Burke
Making Sense of Church: Eavesdropping on Emerging Conversations About God, Community, and Culture—with Colleen Pepper

Larry Crabb
Connecting
The Safest Place on Earth
Shattered Dreams: God's Unexpected Path to Joy
The Pressure's Off: There's a New Way to Live
Soul Talk: The Language God Longs for Us to Speak

Dwight Edwards
Revolution Within: A Fresh Look at Supernatural Living

Stanley J. Grenz
A Primer on Postmodernism
Beyond Foundationalism: Shaping Theology in a Postmodern Context—with John R. Franke
Renewing the Center: Evangelical Theology in a Post-Theological Era
Pocket Dictionary of Theological Terms—with David Guretzki and Cherith Fee Nordling

Darrell L. Guder
> *Missional Church: A Vision for the Sending of the Church in North America*
> *The Continuing Conversion of the Church*

Douglas John Hall
> *The End of Christendom and the Future of Christianity*

George Hunsberger and Craig Van Gelder
> *The Church Between Gospel and Culture: The Emerging Mission in North America*

Jim Kouzes and Barry Posner
> *The Leadership Challenge*
> *Credibility: How Leaders Gain and Lose It, Why People Demand It*
> *Encouraging the Heart: A Leader's Guide to Rewarding and Recognizing Others*

Alan Kreider
> *The Change of Conversion and the Origin of Christendom*

Gordon MacDonald
> *Ordering Your Private World*

Brennan Manning
> *The Ragamuffin Gospel*
> *Abba's Child: The Cry of the Heart for Intimate Belonging*
> *Ruthless Trust: The Ragamuffin's Path to God*

Brian McLaren
> *The Church on the Other Side*
> *A New Kind of Christian: A Tale of Two Friends on a Spiritual Journey*
> *The Story We Find Ourselves In: Further Adventures of a New Kind of Christian*
> *A Is for Abductive: The Language of the Emerging Church—* with Leonard Sweet and Jerry Haselmayer
> *More Ready Than You Realize: Evangelism As Dance in the Postmodern Matrix*

Bruce McNicol and Bill Thrall

The Ascent of a Leader: How Ordinary Relationships Develop Extraordinary Character and Influence—with Ken McElrath

TrueFaced: Trust God and Others with Who You Really Are—with John Lynch

Loren B. Mead

The Once and Future Church: Reinventing the Congregation for a New Mission Frontier

Calvin Miller

The Sermon Maker: Tales of a Transformed Preacher

Donald Miller

Blue Like Jazz: Nonreligious Thoughts on Christian Spirituality

Lesslie Newbigin

The Open Secret: An Introduction to the Theology of Mission

The Gospel in a Pluralist Society

Foolishness to the Greeks: The Gospel and Western Culture

Mission in Christ's Way: A Gift, a Command, an Assurance

Henri J. M. Nouwen

In The Name of Jesus: Reflections on Christian Leadership

The Return of the Prodigal Son: A Story of Homecoming

Eugene Peterson

Working the Angles: The Shape of Pastoral Integrity

Five Smooth Stones for Pastoral Work

Under the Unpredictable Plant: An Exploration in Vocational Holiness

The Unnecessary Pastor: Rediscovering the Call—with Marva Dawn

Mike Regele

Death of the Church—with Mark Schulz

Alan J. Roxburgh

The Missionary Congregation, Leadership, and Liminality

Ronald J. Sider, Philip Olson, and Heidi Rolland Unruh
>
> *Churches That Make a Difference: Reaching Your Community with Good News and Good Works*

Leonard Sweet
>
> *Post-Modern Pilgrims: First Century Passion for the 21st Century World*
>
> *SoulTsunami: Sink or Swim in New Millennium Culture*

Barbara Brown Taylor
>
> *When God Is Silent*

Craig Van Gelder
>
> *The Essence of the Church: A Community Created by the Spirit*

Robert E. Webber
>
> *The Younger Evangelicals: Facing the Challenges of the New World*
>
> *Ancient-Future Faith: Rethinking Evangelicalism for a Postmodern World*
>
> *Journey to Jesus: The Worship, Evangelism, and Nurture Mission of the Church*
>
> *The Book of Daily Prayer*

Dallas Willard
>
> *The Spirit of the Disciplines: Understanding How God Changes Lives*
>
> *The Divine Conspiracy: Rediscovering Our Hidden Life in God*
>
> *Renovation of the Heart: Putting on the Character of Christ*
>
> *Hearing God: Developing a Conversational Relationship with God*

Websites not to miss:
>
> In exploring these websites, please pay attention to the links that each suggests.
>
> www.ancientfutureworship.com
>
> www.crcc.org
>
> www.emergentvillage.com

www.gocn.org
www.iancron.com
www.kendavis.com (Dynamic Communicators Workshop)
www.leadershipcatalyst.org
www.leadershipdesigngroup.org
www.lifeenrichment.org
www.newwayministries.org (School of Spiritual Direction;
    Soul Care Conference)
www.newbigin.net
www.the-next-wave.org
www.stanleyjgrenz.com
www.theooze.com

Acknowledgments

Wes Roberts

Beginning with our triune God, I want to give him all the thanks he deserves for the sacred privilege of this project. It has been a consistent delight to work with Glenn Marshall. What a brilliant and good-hearted man. What a faithful shepherd in a small but powerful place. And I thank Nanci McAlister, formerly of NavPress, for inviting us to do this book. Special kudos go to our assigned editor, Brad Lewis, for all we've learned from you. Thank you for hanging in there with us. We know we put you through your paces. Profound thanks goes to Kathy Mosier, Nicci Jordan, Terry Behimer, and Dan Rich, all of NavPress, for their strong, creative encouragement and belief in this project.

Among many valued friends, who have also been a rich resource of encouragement, are the growing and authentic people with whom we have a unique and strong bond in our small group: Tom and Jenny Board, Larry and Rachael Crabb, and Bob and Claudia Ingram. And I am thankful for the continued support of the board of directors of Leadership Design Group/Life Enrichment: Ron and Cindy Baldwin (now retired from the board), Gary and Jorie Gulbranson, Marc and Marsha McBride, Tim and Janean Stripe, and Dick and Bo Teodoro.

I am also indebted to a number of the younger, curious, daring,

creative, radical, emerging leaders with whom I get to "hang out" from time to time. Some of these men and women are much younger in age than this "wild old man." Others are closer to where I live in the years of life. All are vibrant in spirit and have experienced some of the transforming realities of life. And all have taught me much through their own lives as they have allowed me to walk with them over many profound, heartfelt, developmental, and sacred paths in recent months: Creighton and Nikki Alexander, Brian Aycock, Mark Beach, Barbara Booker, Mike Bourque, Vance Brown, Angi Crane, Michael Cusick, Matt Dealy, Curtis Feltcher, Chris Haggerty, Aaron Lessig, Ken Lynn, Steve and Elaine Musick, Brian Pikalow, Joy Sawyer, Jason Smith, Paul Stolwyk, Dennis and Cathy Turner, McNair Wilson, Dave Wayman, and Mike Worley.

I owe a significant debt of gratitude to Bill and Jennifer Nath for allowing Judy and me to spend a generous chunk of time at their place in Arizona as the first major draft of this book was formed in November 2002. And a huge thanks goes to Bob and Mitzi Beach, who allowed us to recover from the rigors of writing and our life work at their "Beach Dream" in March 2003. What you two couples provided was a most necessary and timely gift of space and place. Thank you.

Much gratitude also goes to my mother-in-law, Alice Sutter, who asks about "the book" every time we phone her or visit her in person. (In the summer of 2003, she is living in a nursing home in Phoenix and is fast approaching ninety-nine years old in November.) She has been the best! My bride since 1967, Judy, and my daughter since 1976, Shannon, have been the essence of encouragement and often lively debate on the issues of life. I continue to learn more about God's grace-filled love through them than anyone else on the planet. How I thank our triune God for you two!

Glenn Marshall

There are many people whom I would like to recognize for their help and encouragement on this project. First, I want to give my sincere thanks to Wes Roberts for asking me to be involved. Wes is a rare gem. He is someone who is willing to think deeply about the practical aspects of the Christian faith. He is beyond brilliant—he has wisdom. His radical faith, humility, and devotion to the Lord have been a constant example to me. Wes, it has been a real joy to work on this project with you. Thanks for bringing me on board.

More than a few words of gratitude need to given to the good people of Park Avenue Community Church in Somerdale, New Jersey, for sparing me the time to do this work. Your many words of encouragement and your prayers have been a constant source of strength. You have put up with my foibles now for almost twelve years. I thank the Lord for the privilege of being your pastor.

For my unpaid staff at the church, Reggie Dawson and Angela Davidson, I give you my sincere thanks—not only for your encouragement on this project, but also for your everyday service and dedication to the Lord Jesus. Each day that you serve with joy is an inspiration to me. Words cannot express my gratitude for you.

To my good friend Gary Westra, who provided me a place at his campsite to get away and write and wrestled with me about much of this material, thanks for your hospitality, for lending me your books, and for trying to keep me straight. Thanks for your input during those campfire ponderings. I hope you will see some of our discussions represented here.

Thanks also to Bob Hopper, who graciously conceded to take the chair of our presbytery's Church Development Committee so that I might concentrate more fully on this project.

And finally, for my family I give thanks to the Lord. For my daughter, Colleen, who continues to be a source of joy, I thank the Lord for his grace in your life. And for my son, Jeremy, whose discussions about postmodernism have kept me on my toes. Thank you, son, for your input. And finally for my wife, Jackie, who put up with my musings and mutterings for the past several months and allowed me space to write—whatever I say will be inadequate to express my thankfulness for you. You are God's gift to me.

About the Authors

WES ROBERTS is the author of *Support Your Local Pastor* and founder/CCO of Leadership Design Group/Life Enrichment, a worldwide ministry of mentoring, consulting, and counseling to Christian leaders. He holds a B.S. in Christian education from Biola University and an M.A. in pastoral counseling from Denver Seminary. Wes lives in Parker, Colorado, with his wife, Judy. They have one daughter.

GLENN MARSHALL pastors Park Avenue Community Church, a congregation of about seventy members, in Somerdale, New Jersey. He and his wife, Jackie, have a son and a daughter.

You may contact Wes at:
Leadership Design Group/Life Enrichment
17053 Hastings Avenue
Parker, CO 80134
Phone: (303) 840-4371
Fax: (303) 840-4372
E-mail: ldgle@earthlink.net
Websites: www.leadershipdesigngroup.org
www.lifeenrichment.org